The GALLIPOLI SERIES

PAINTINGS BY GEOFF HARVEY

Text by Ion Idriess

ETT IMPRINT
Exile Bay

First published by ETT Imprint, Exile Bay 2022

To coincide with the artist's exhibition at Robin Gibson Galleries April 2022

Extracts from *The Desert Column* by Ion Idriess (ETT Imprint 2017)

ETT IMPRINT
PO Box R1906
Royal Exchange NSW 1225 Australia

ISBN 978-1-922698-22-3 (paper)
ISBN 978-1-922698-24-7 (ebook)

Edited and design by Tom Thompson

Cover: *Enlisting*, by Geoff Harvey

THE PAINTINGS

THE PAINTINGS

The
GALLIPOLI SERIES

The "Desert Column" is more than my diary. It is myself, I began the diary as we crowded the decks off Gallipoli and watched the first shells crash into Turkish soil...The diary was a very young soldier's idea. He thought that if he survived shot and shell and sickness, he would like, when he came to be an old man, to be able to read exactly what his feelings were when "things were happening." Have a private picture show all his own, as it were, to refresh his memory.

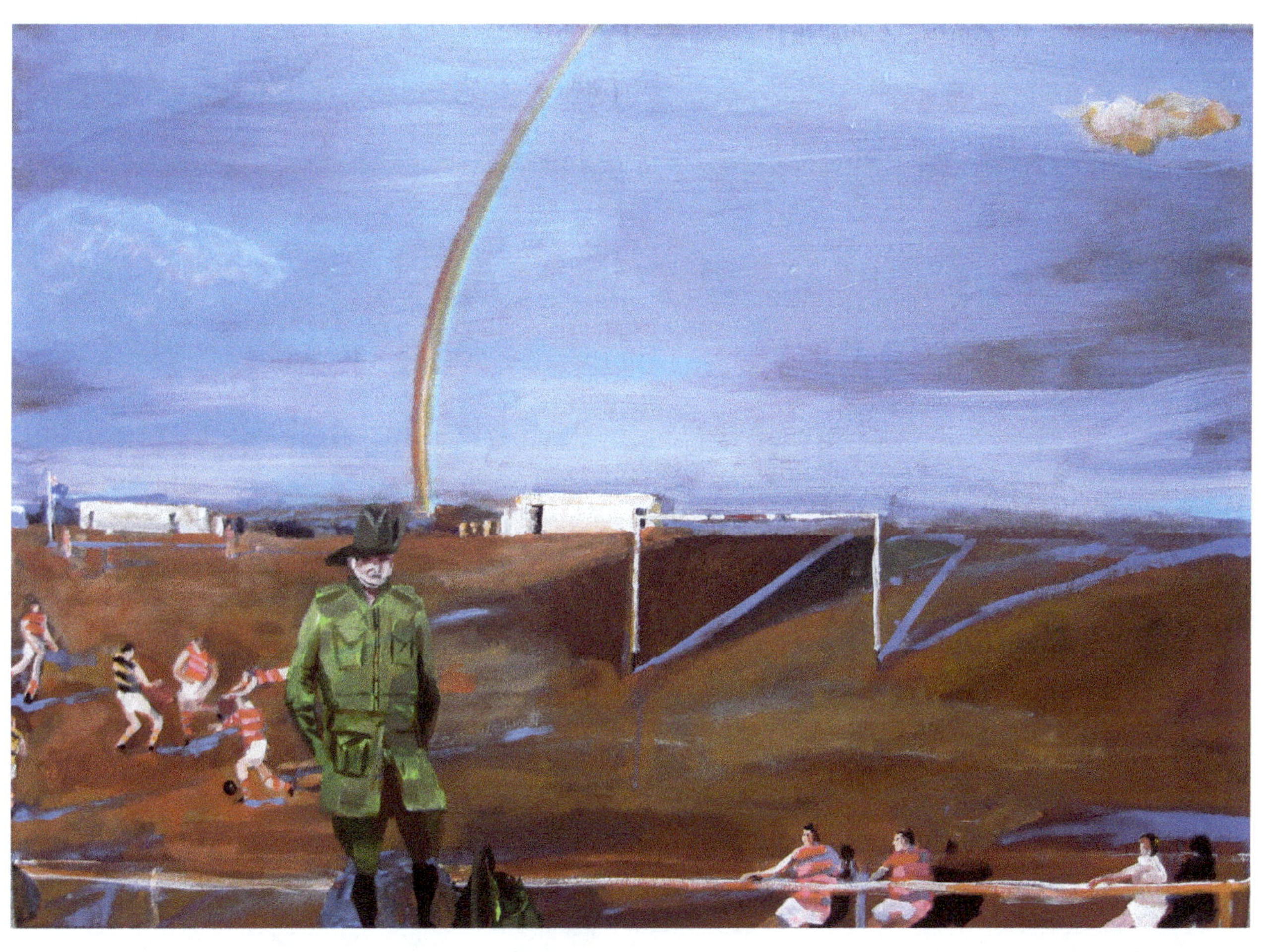

"Too young for war"

80 x 110 cm

acrylic on board

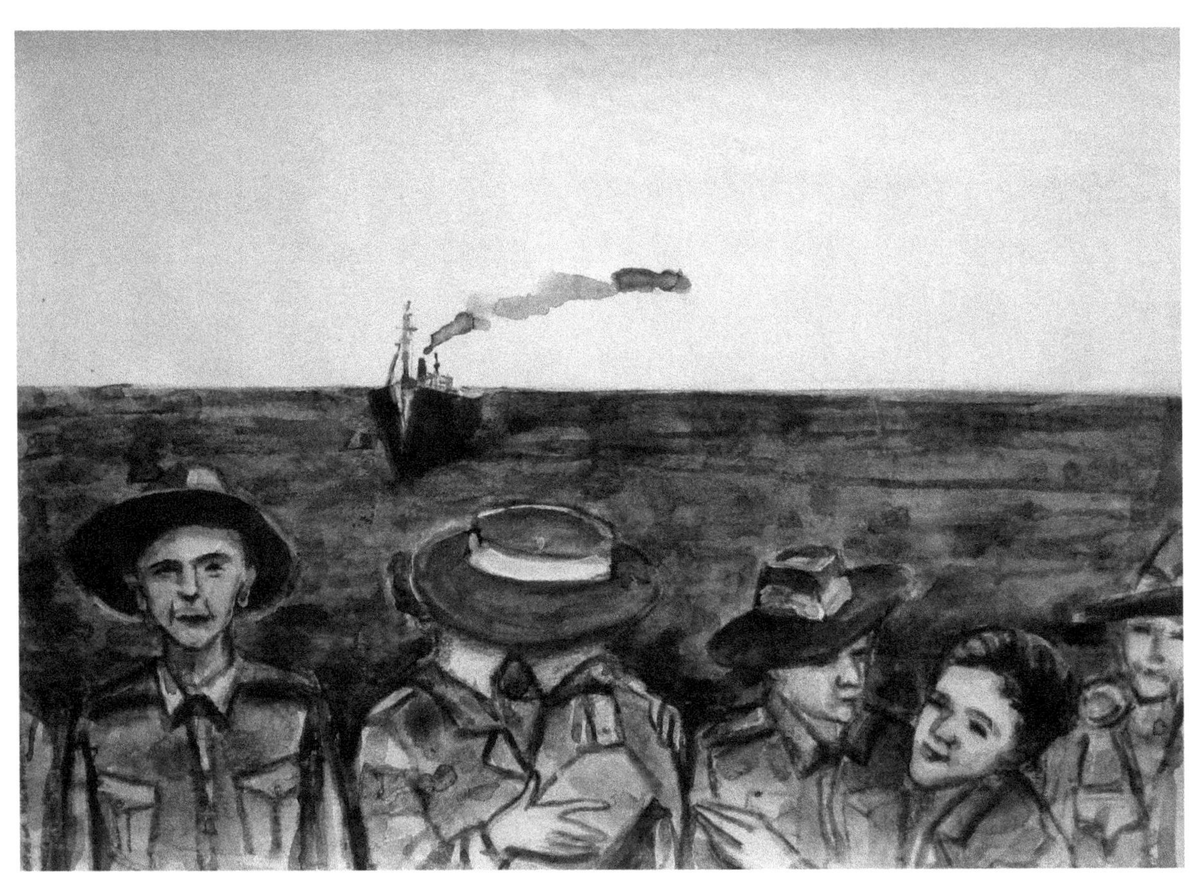

Farewell Embrace
42 x 5 cm
Ink on paper

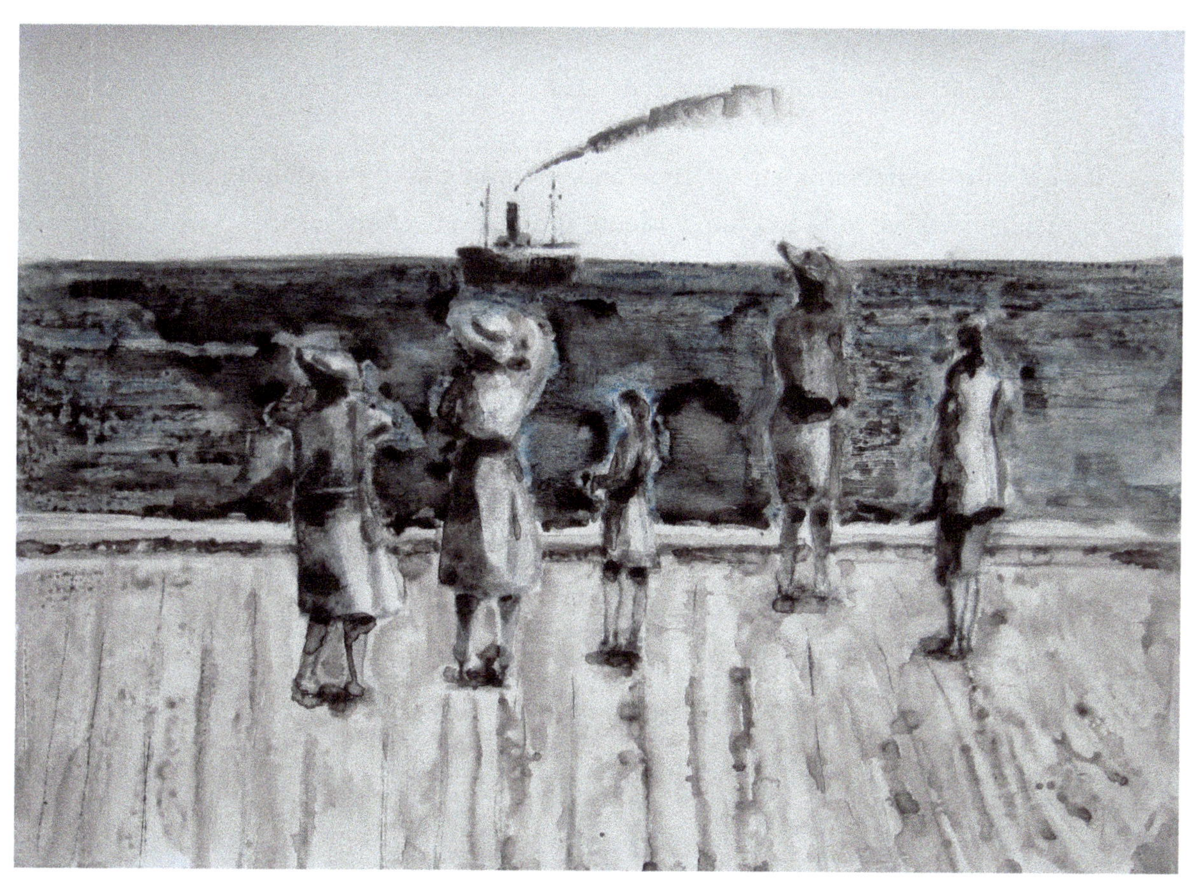

Goodbye
42 x 57 cm
ink on paper

Any old date—Sand, sand, sand, flying sand, blooming sand everywhere. Sometimes we have to sit in camp with our greatcoats over our heads. Some days it is impossible to see the length of the horse lines for flying sand.

...The Turks have not come yet, worse luck. Anything to relieve this cursed monotony and sand. Yesterday was awful. In the evening I was riding from the canal, with three led horses prancing with the pain of driving sand in their eyes. I couldn't see five yards ahead. Presently I realized we must have passed the camp, So as the horses persistently tugged to the right I let them try their luck. We pranced right into the sickhorse lines. I had been making right out into the open desert.

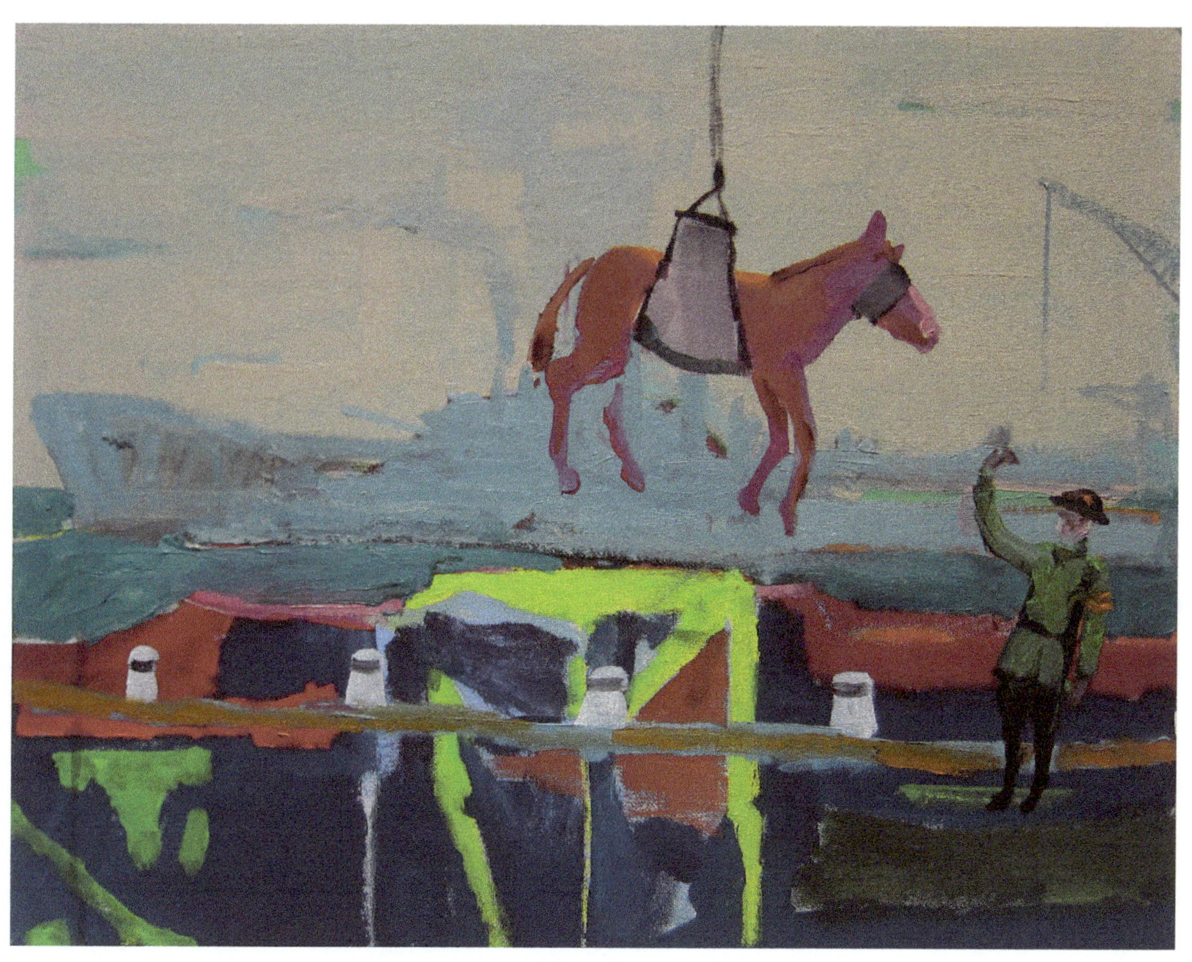

Loading the Walers
41 x 51 cm
acrylic on canvas board

June 28th—Here I am, in Alexandria, growling as usual, tired of having been in bed so long. The old leg, under efficient treatment, healed rapidly, but it seems to have broken out again. I employed the time lying here by thinking out a couple of war inventions. I forwarded the plans to the Brigadier and to Admiral Robinson. Naturally I got no reply. However, it helped time pass.

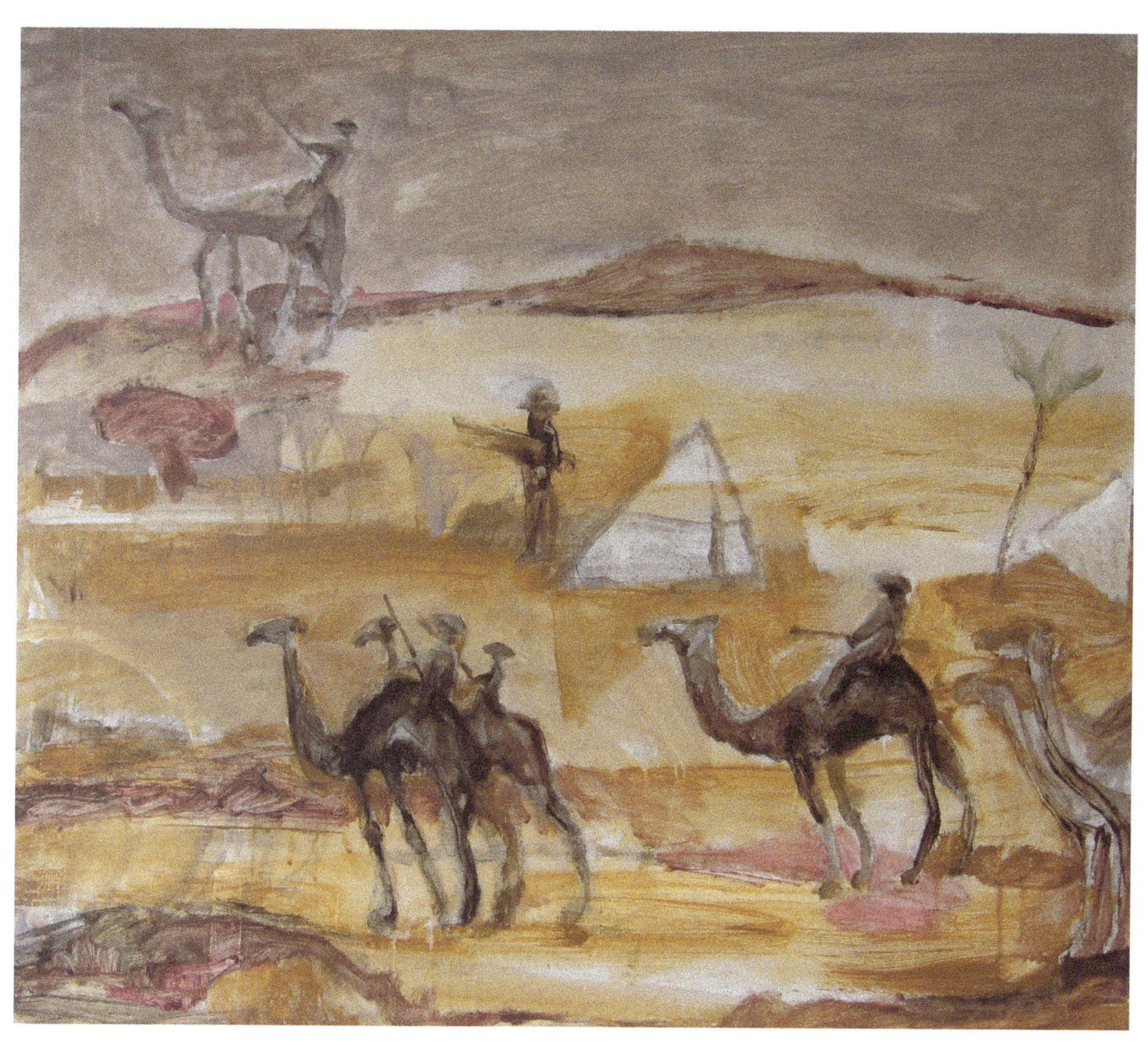

Training in Egypt
41 x 41 cm
acrylic on board

As their thousands grew the rhythm thumped up to us—tramp, tramp, tramp, tramp. We gazed down on the closely packed ranks—they looked so well, so fit, so clean, altogether splendid. The rumble of their guns was a hoarse muttering—clink of chains—gleam of wheels—guns, guns, guns Splendid horses, shiny harness, polished chains, rumble, rumble, rumble, and ammunition columns coming, coming, coming! Parallel were their transport columns, and all the Camel Corps of Egypt seemed lurching red over the skyline.

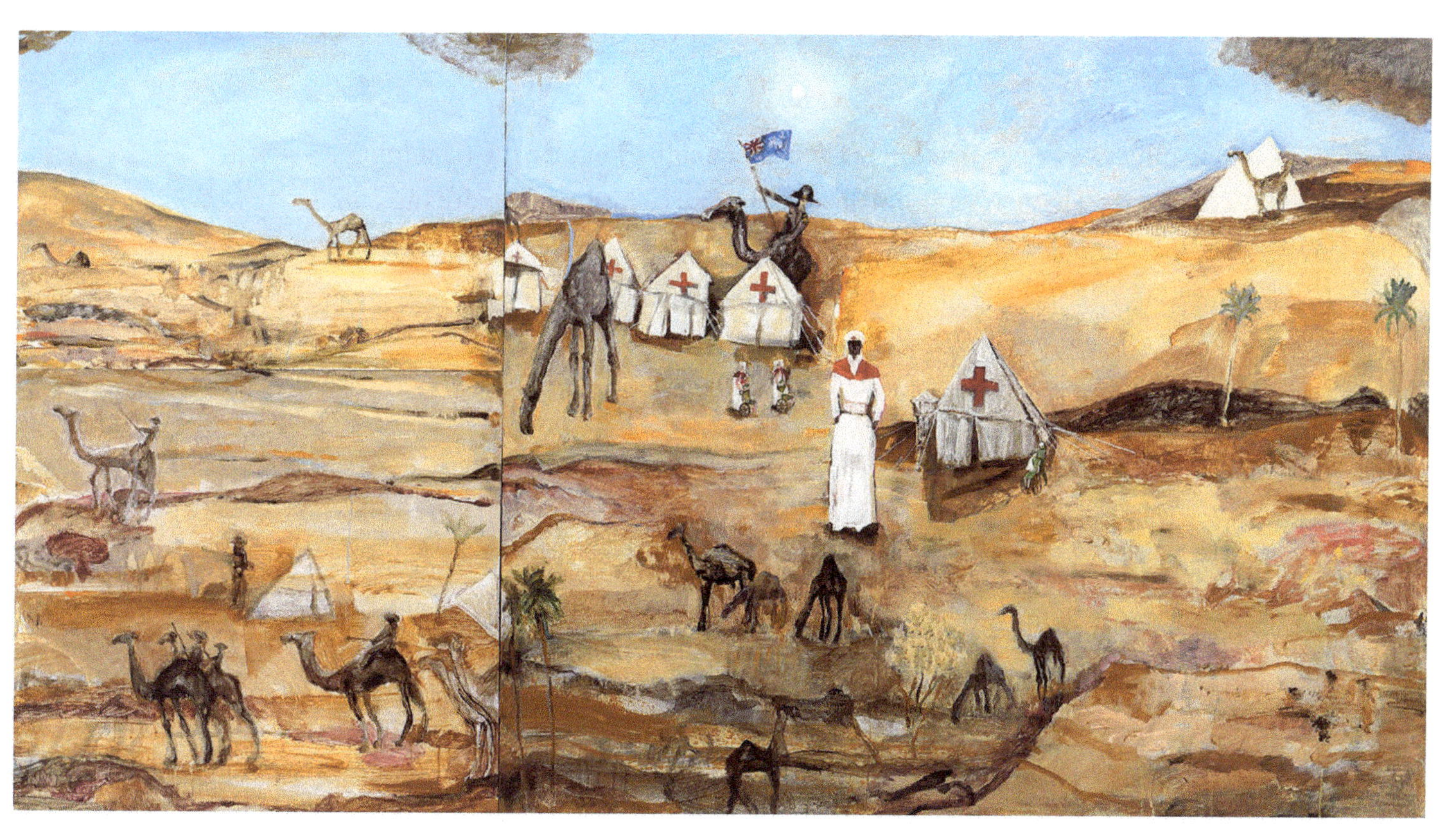

Sister Kelly and the first Imperial Camel Corp Brigade
108 x 190 cm
acrylic on board

The minesweeper is standing by. We are re-embarking for the final four hours' trip. There was a storm at sea last night. This morning driving rain and mist temporarily blot out the shipping. The rough sea looks cold. We hope it. is not raining on the Peninsula for the cold there is intense.

Under Cover of Darkness
160 x 100 cm
oil on canvas

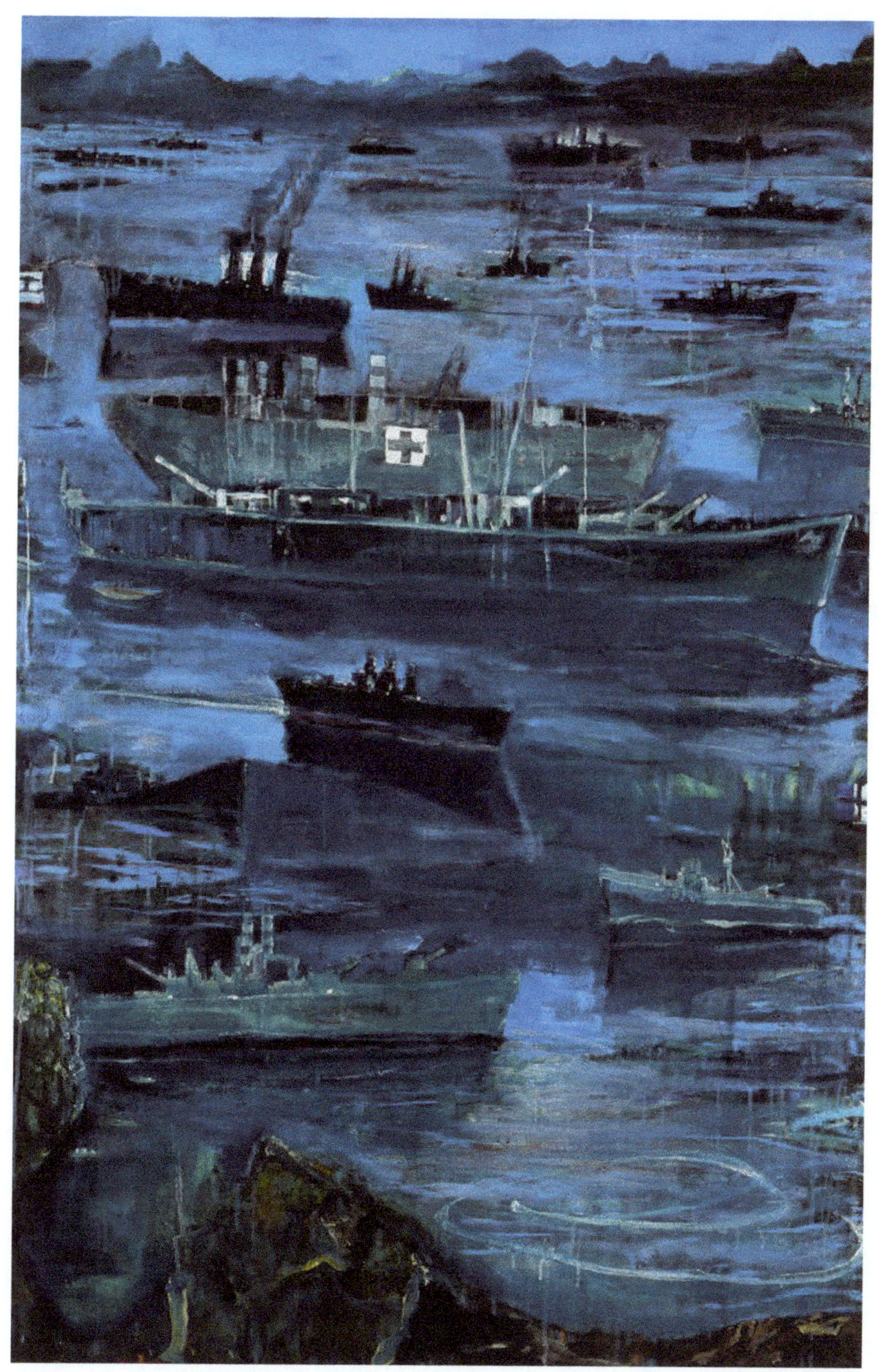

…One of the Turkish shells has just struck a destroyer loaded with troops. Luckily it only killed two and wounded ten. The troops are landing—jumping from the boats in a wading plunge to the beach. The shrapnel is exploding above them—their backs are bent as they run across the beach seeking shelter.

The snipers shot seventeen of our men to-day in one spot alone in the gully.

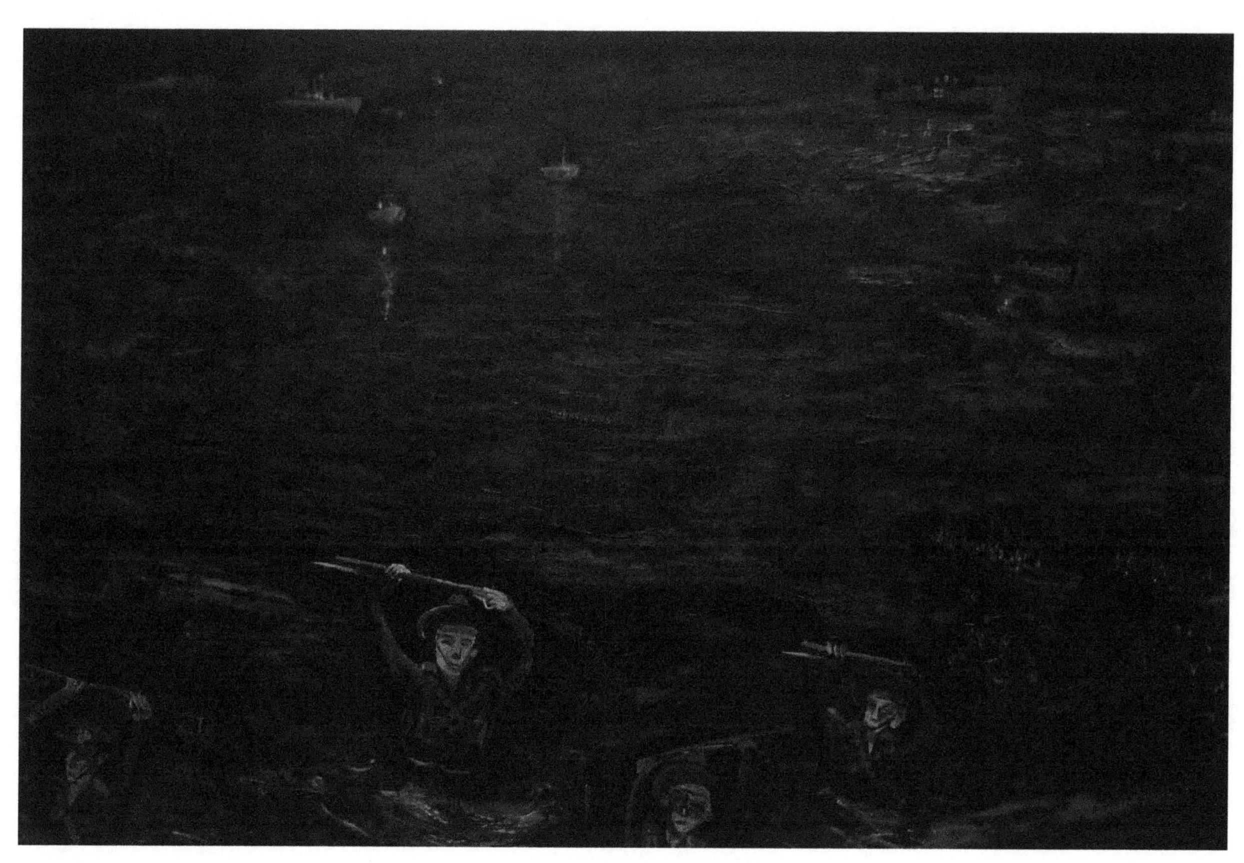

The Landing
82 x 120 cm
acrylic on board

Overhead screamed the big shells from our own guns, travelling towards the Turks and they were shrilled in chorus by the Turkish shells as they criss-crossed down into us. The shells made hell's row in the dark and when exploding close dazzled our eyes with sheets of flame. Jagged fragments screamed into the bushes or struck rocks and screeched piercingly away. My body was alertly passive, but the mind was curiously thinking, "So this is War!"

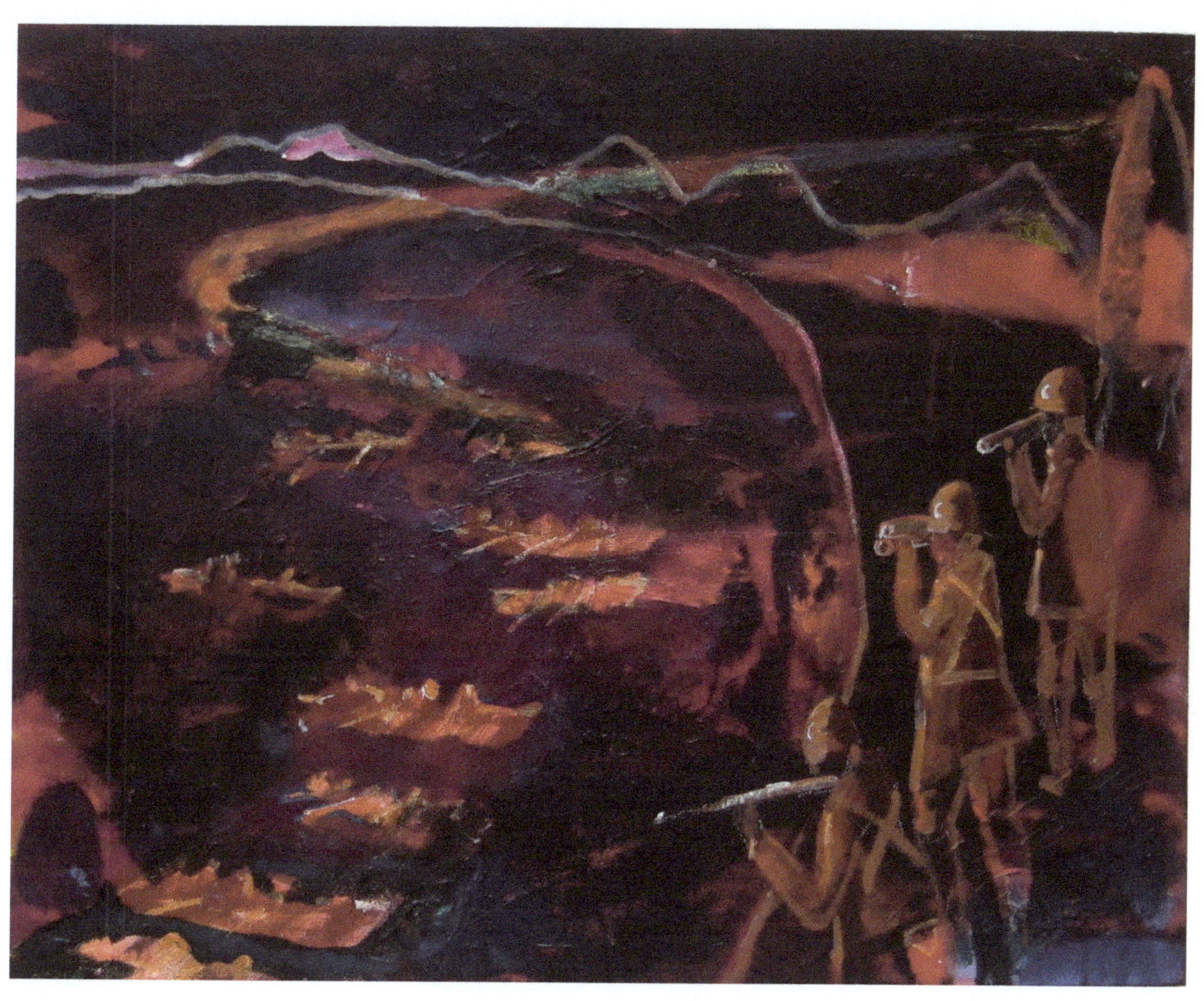

Turks Witness the Landing
41 x 51 cm
acrylic on canvas board

And so we climbed the back of the big hill that faces the sea. We are digging holes to get in out of the way of the shrapnel. Quite close one of our hidden Australian guns replies to the Turks and makes a monstrous row. The steep hills are covered with a dense, prickly shrub.

...We have just been called to arms. I suppose we are going into the trenches.

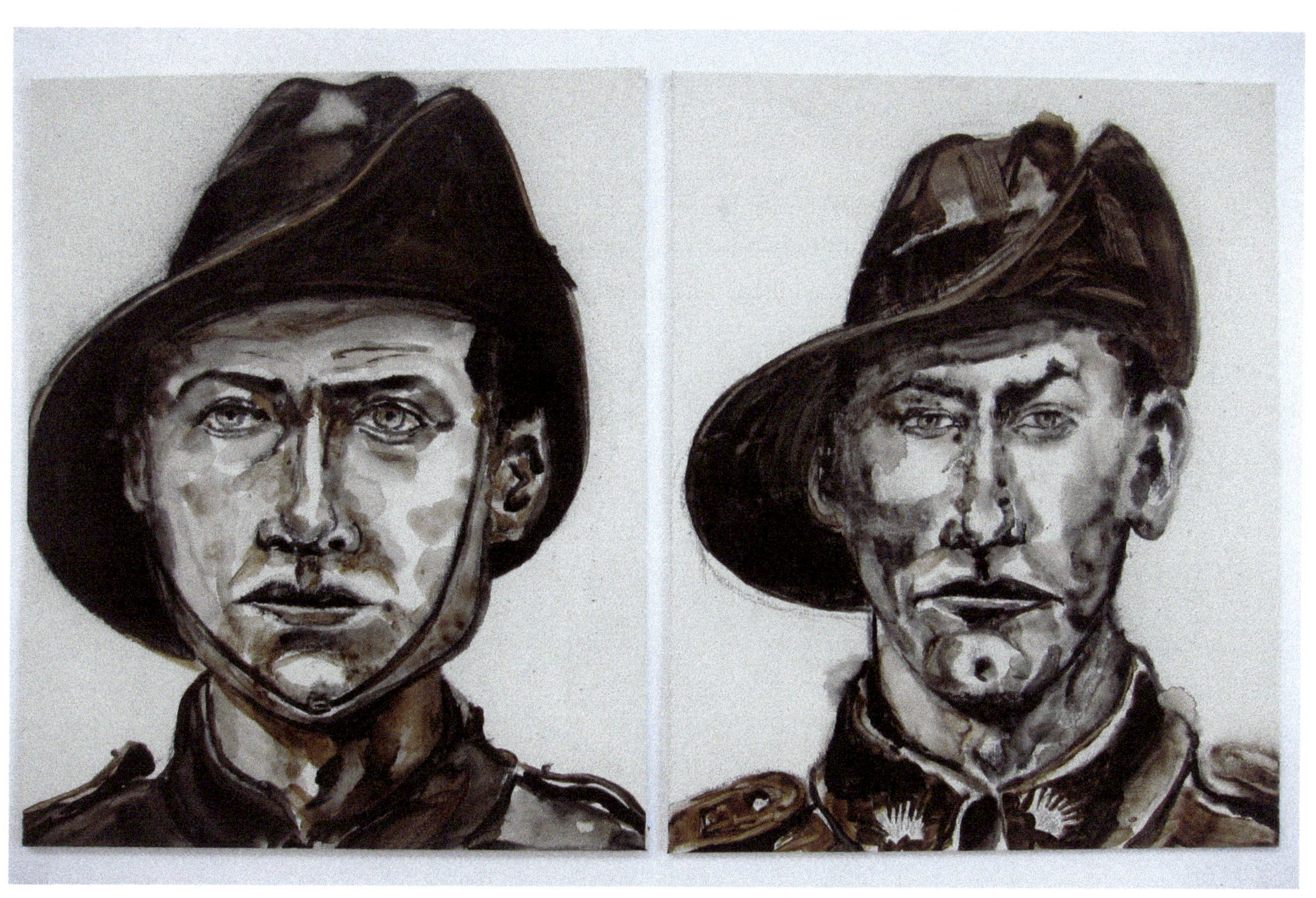

Young Men
41 x 51 cm
acrylic on canvas board

This morning five thousand Turks are lying before the Australian trenches. There were a hundred and twenty seven men and four officers of the First Light Horse Brigade killed. The infantry casualties we do not know.

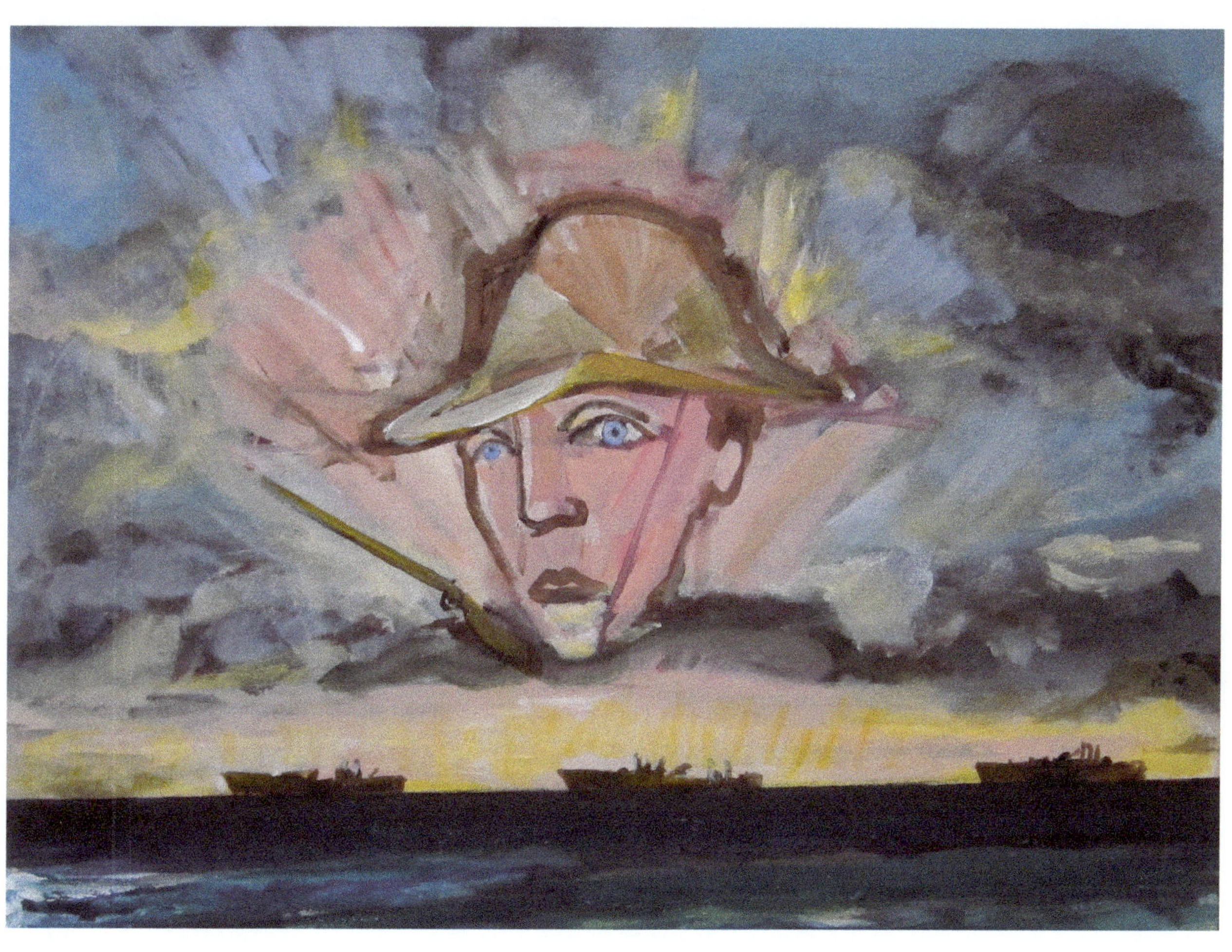

First Light
41 x 51 cm
acrylic on canvas board

The shrapnel is bursting directly in front of that landing crowd now—from here it appears to be exploding above the first hill. Apparently the Turkish gunners cannot quite get the range. What ho—she bumps! A shell has crashed right into their boat! What a lovely time is awaiting us!

Our landing-party is ready. What oiling of rifles; excitement; laughing and swearing … Here come the destroyers, racing back hell for leather for more loads. Looks as if men are at a premium.

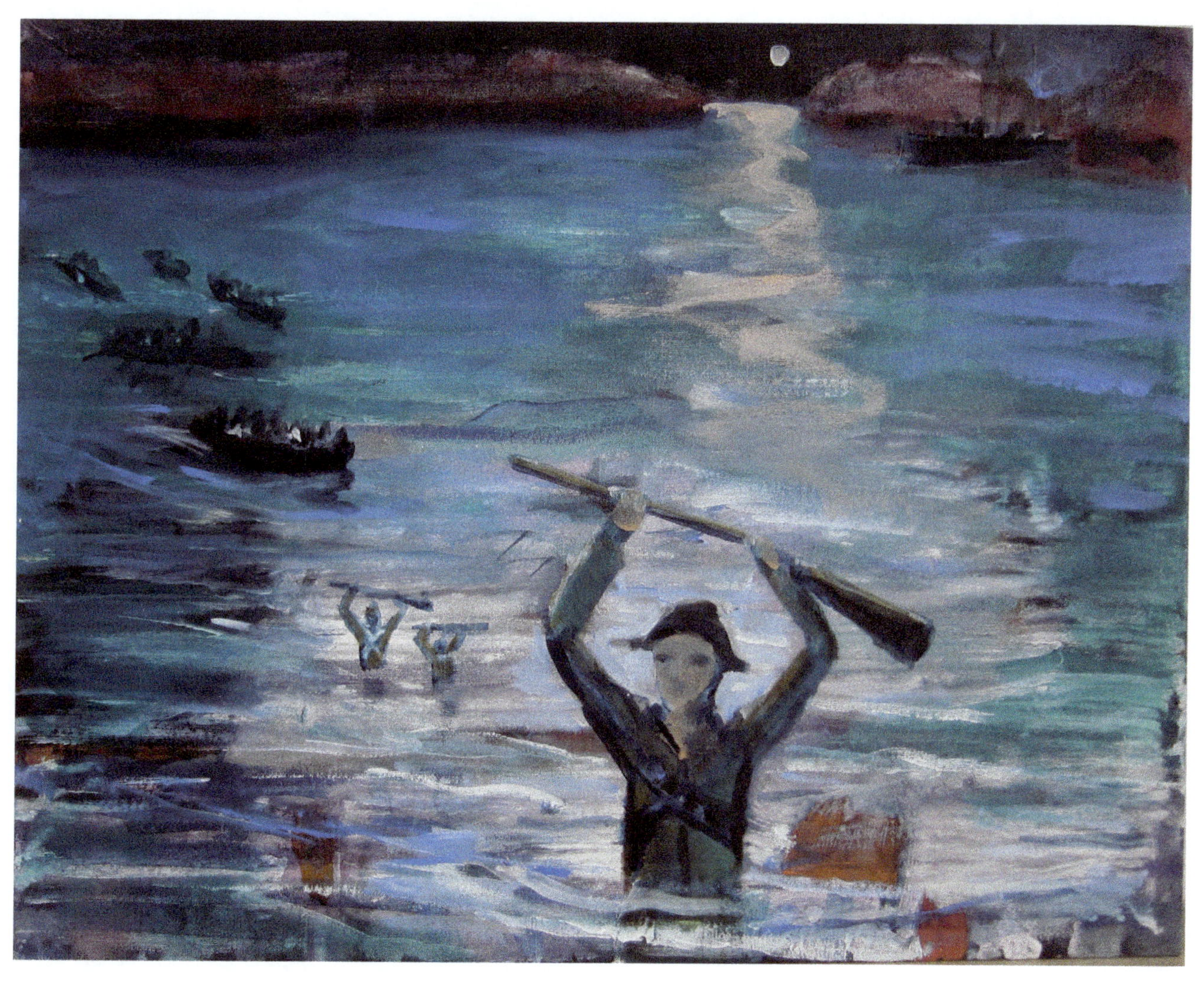

Early Morning 25 April 1915
41 x 51 cm
acrylic on canvas board

We can see the shore distinctly, where our first battalions made Australian history.

What a seemingly impossible task they were set! The landing-place looks a sheer line of rocky cliffs, the abrupt hills frowning under their grey undergrowth. Cliffs and hills and gullies were swarming with Turks and machine guns at the Landing. It must have been a supreme bayonet charge, as awful as its success was miraculous.

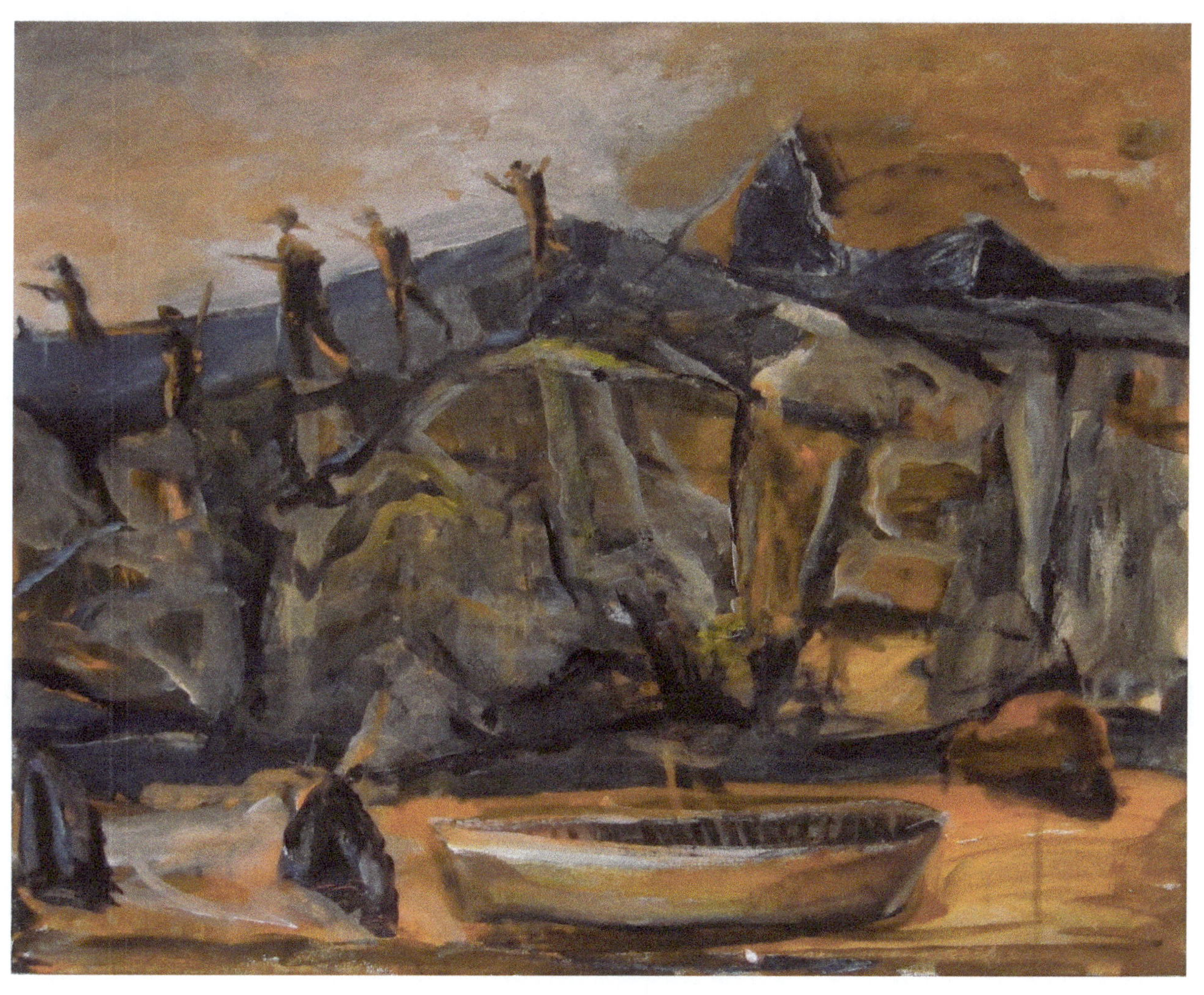

Rough Terrain Landing
41 x 51 cm
acrylic on canvas board

Straight up from the cliff's black edge there rocketed skywards two flaring bombs. They descended directly into the Turkish trenches.
For breathless seconds the rifle-fire ceased, then came a tearing roar that shook the very ground. In streaks of blackened flame there spewed up a smoke-cloud blacker than the night. Some Turks were panic-stricken.
In inky silhouette we glimpsed them, like toy men, away up on the cliffs as they sprang from their trenches to run. But the air vibrated to the machine-gun and rifle-fire that was turned on them.
And thus the game went on all through the night.

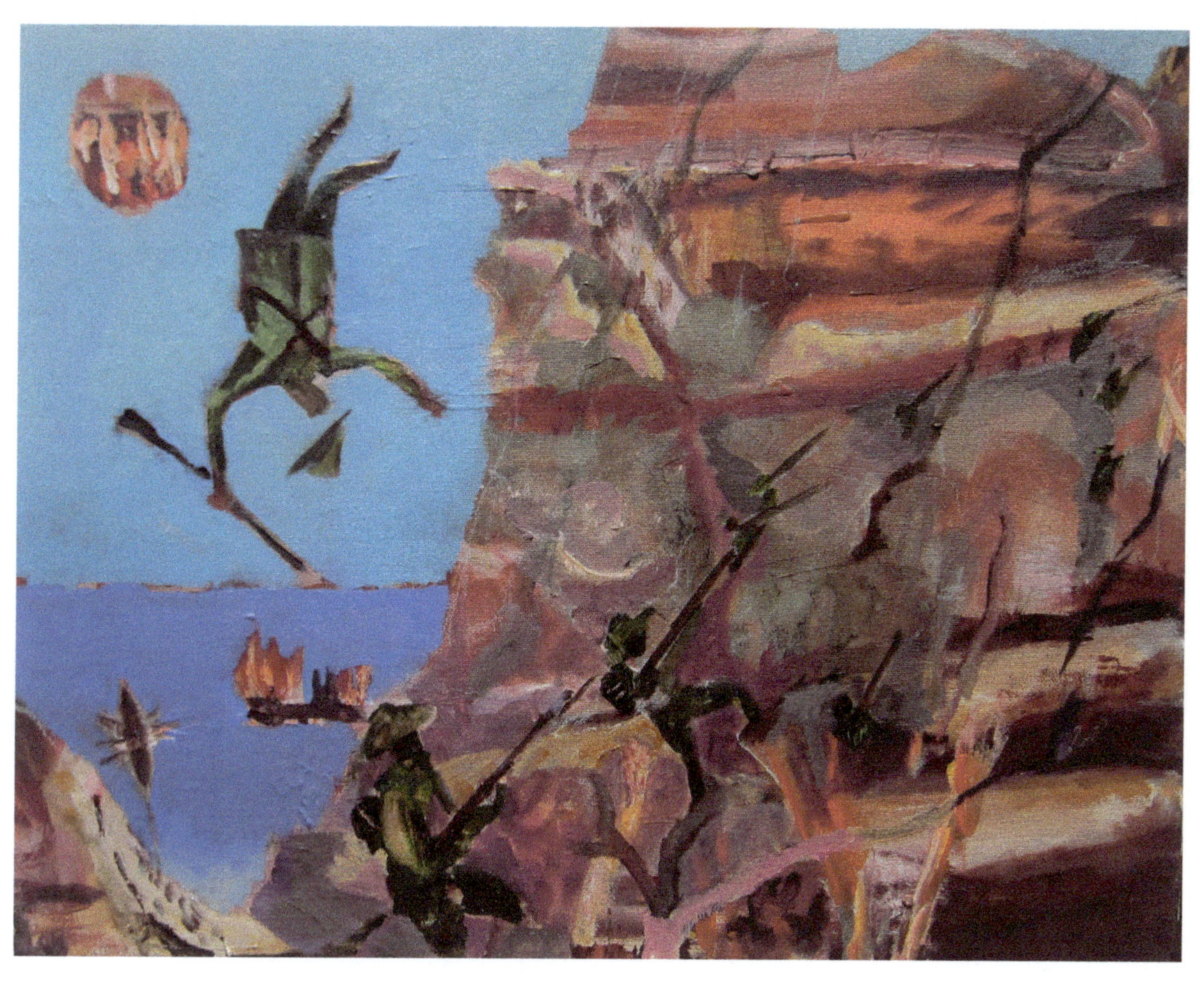

Fallen Trooper
41 x 51 cm
acrylic on canvas board.

Last night was very quiet, just desultory firing rippling away down the line into silence. Our trench runs downhill with the barbed wire into the sea. There's a little destroyer that seems to have adopted the regiment, as a terrier does a man. Last night it sneaked in again, blazed away hell and fury at the Turkish trenches just opposite us, then whipped around and faded into the night as silently as she had come.

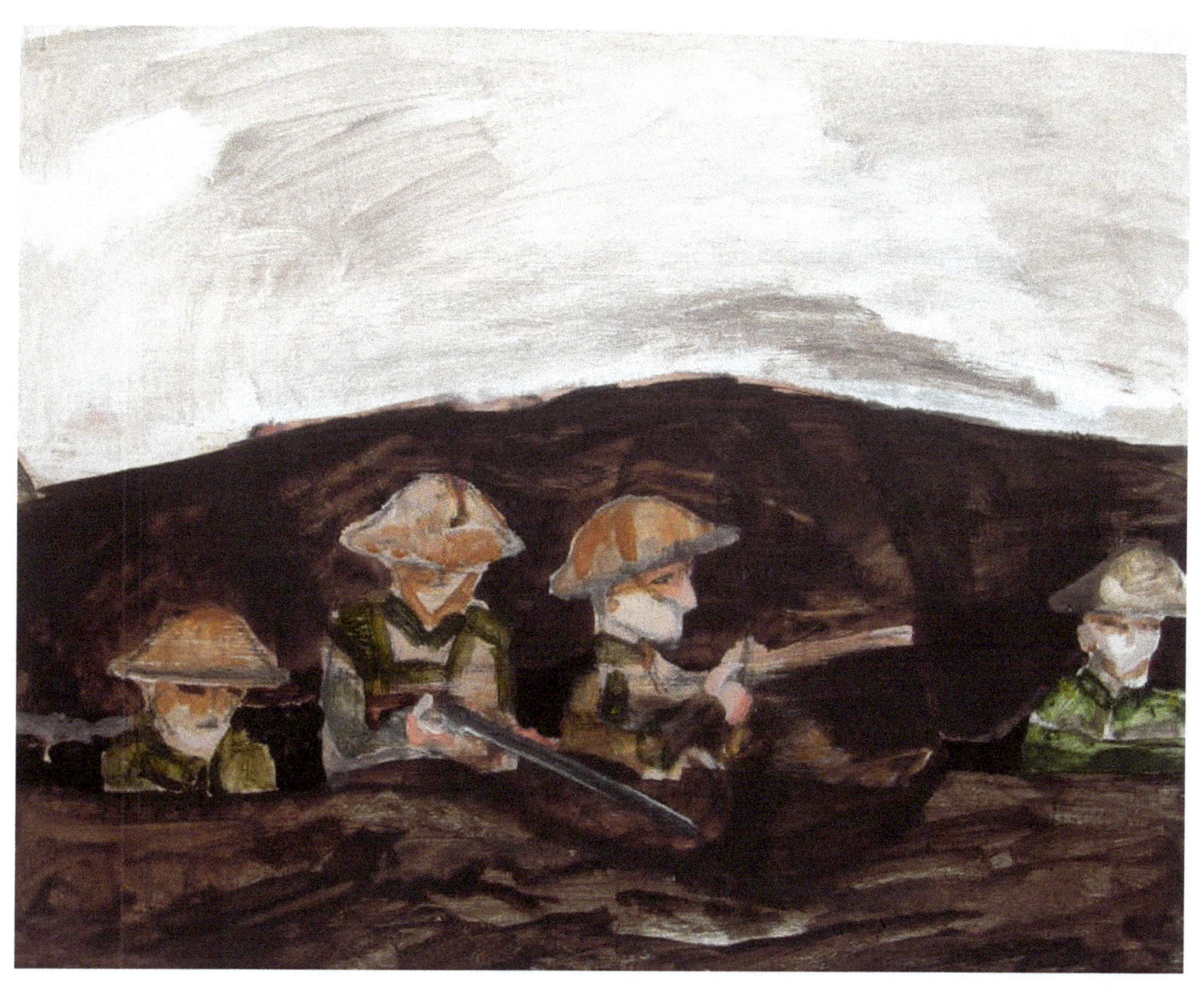

Digging in
41 x 51 cm
acrylic on canvas board

All along the paths leading to and from the trenches are the graves of the Poor Aussies who have been shot. A man grows wary where he walks—many of the graves are so shallow. They could literally call this place "Death's Gully." I've only been here a few hours, but, by Jove, I've seen some dead men. And old dead ones make their presence felt right up and down this great gully.

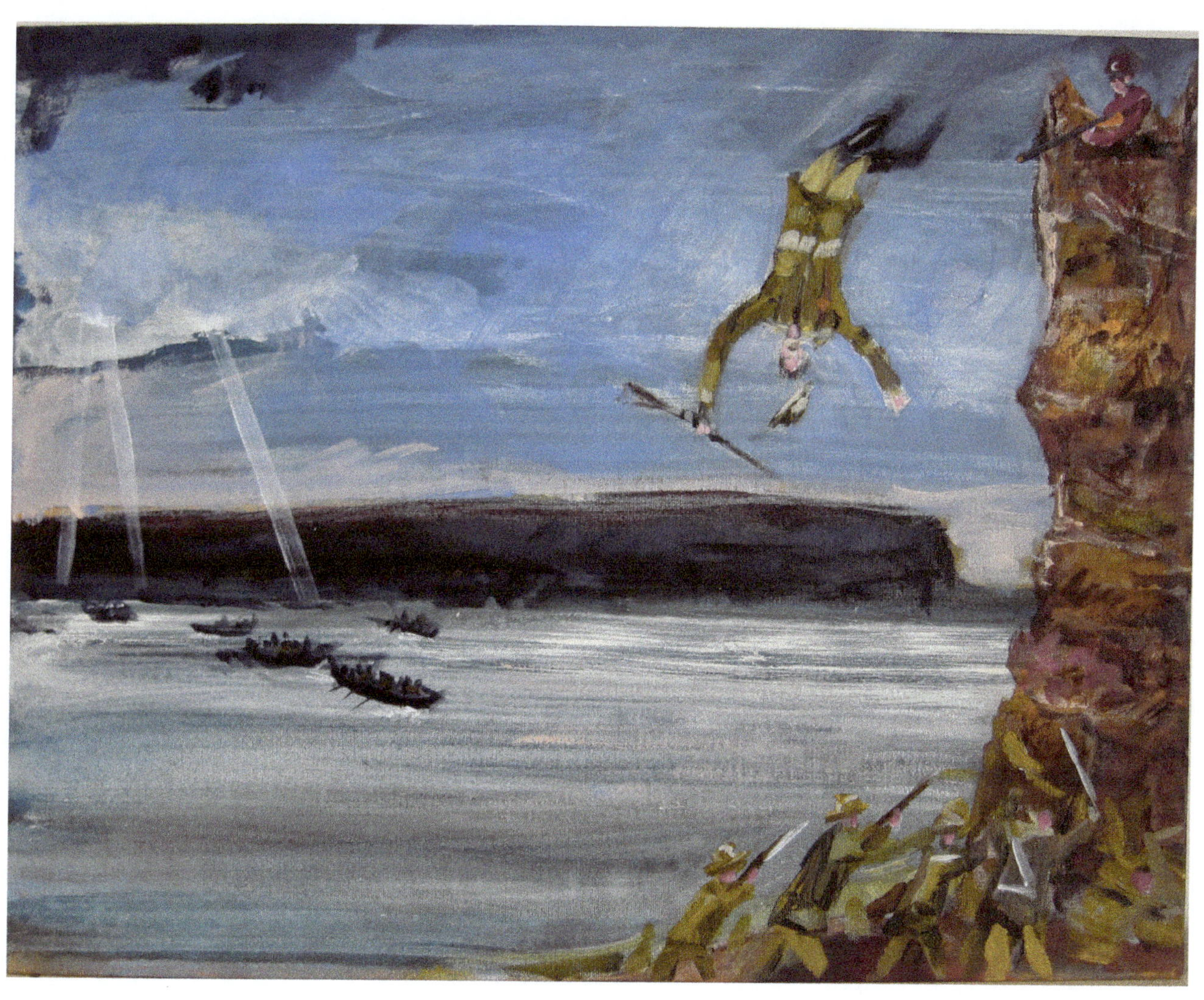

Fierce Fighting
41 x 51 cm
acrylic on canvas board

They took us to the main beach dressing-station where our little lot were attended to and then laid out with the rows of wounded to wait for the day. I sat by King the remainder of the night. I nearly cried sometimes — I was not hurt at all—but those hundreds of poor maimed chaps lying there on the sand were trying to help one another with a joke, a whispered word—a smile—a look.

…In the hospital-ship *Salta.* What a contrast to the *Franconia*!
Long lines of clean bunks, clean tables and chairs and decks, lifts up and down the holds for bringing in the badly wounded. Actually nurses, that smile at a man, and kindly doctors. Fancy getting into a real bed at night! This ship is just heaven.

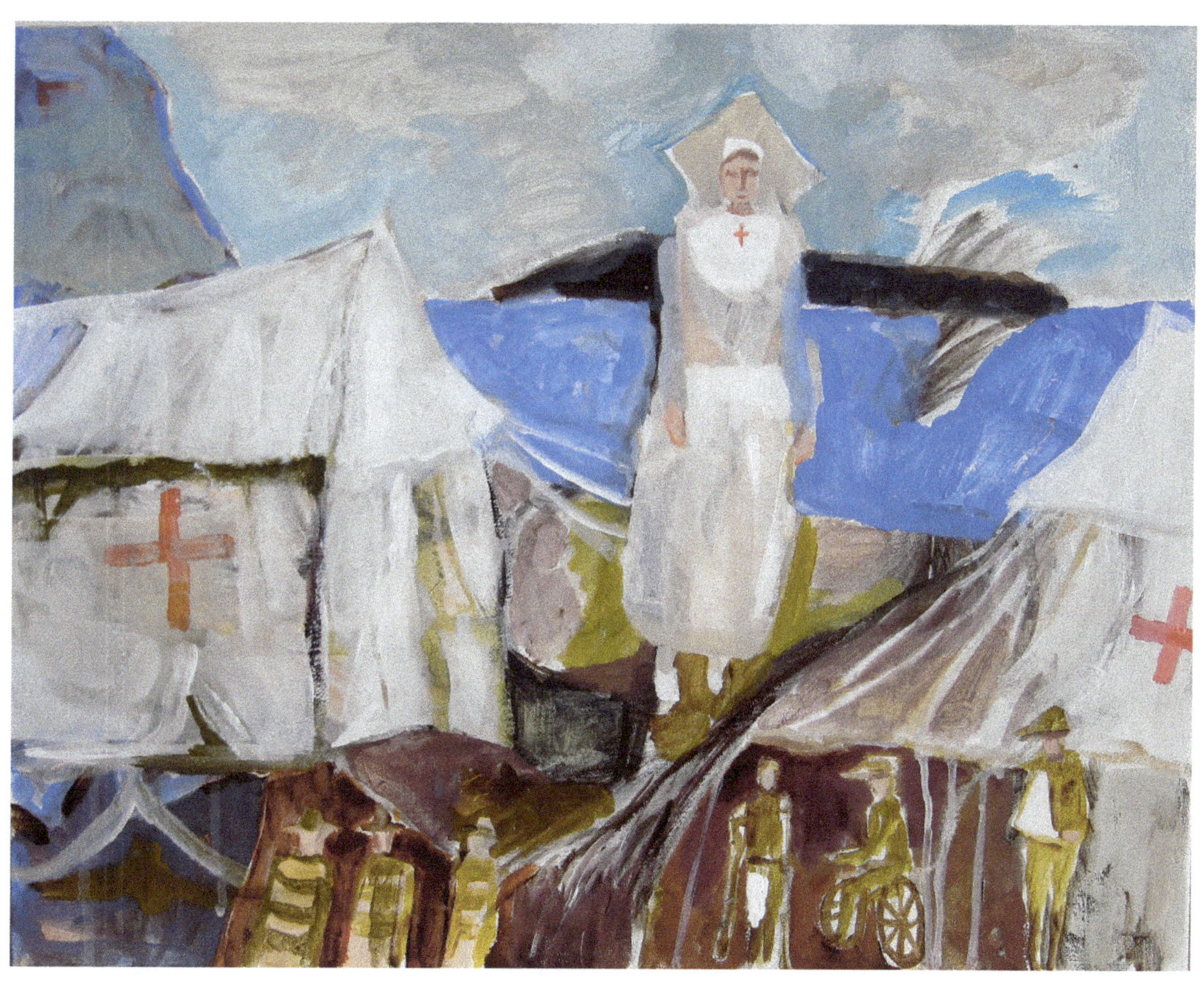

Nurse Kate
41 x 51 cm
acrylic on canvas board

After dinner—The last boatload of men from the other ship has just raced shorewards. They are New Zealanders. As their packed vessels sped by we yelled from our crowded decks the old Cairo sayings: "Sieda! Talla-hena bint!" "Have you got a piastre?" and the pet sayings of the Tommies. They sounded comical with Australian voices imitating the English accents: "Has your mawther got a Ba-by?" "Have you been to Cairo?" etc.

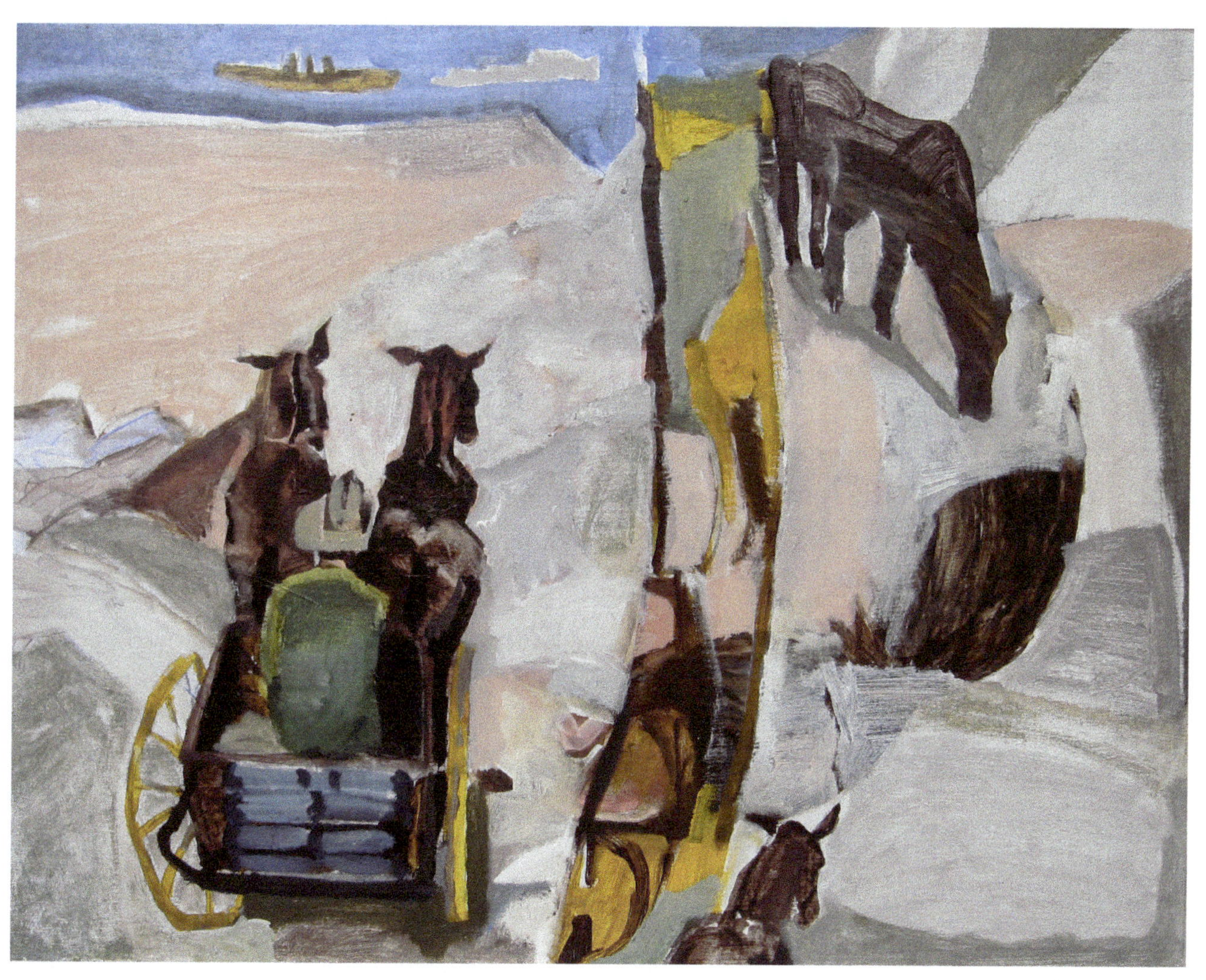

Water Carrier
41 x 51 cm
acrylic on canvas board

We moved off for the shore all ears to the pop, pop, pop of rifle-shots. Smoke fairly belched from the toy funnel: I suppose the sweating devils below were shoving the coal into her.

Nothing happened until we got closer inshore and the bushes on the hillsides began to take shape. Then whizzz, then ping, ping, ping, ping. By jove, rifle-bullets! Whizz-zz, smack! and a shrill receding whistle as the bullet ricocheted off the water.

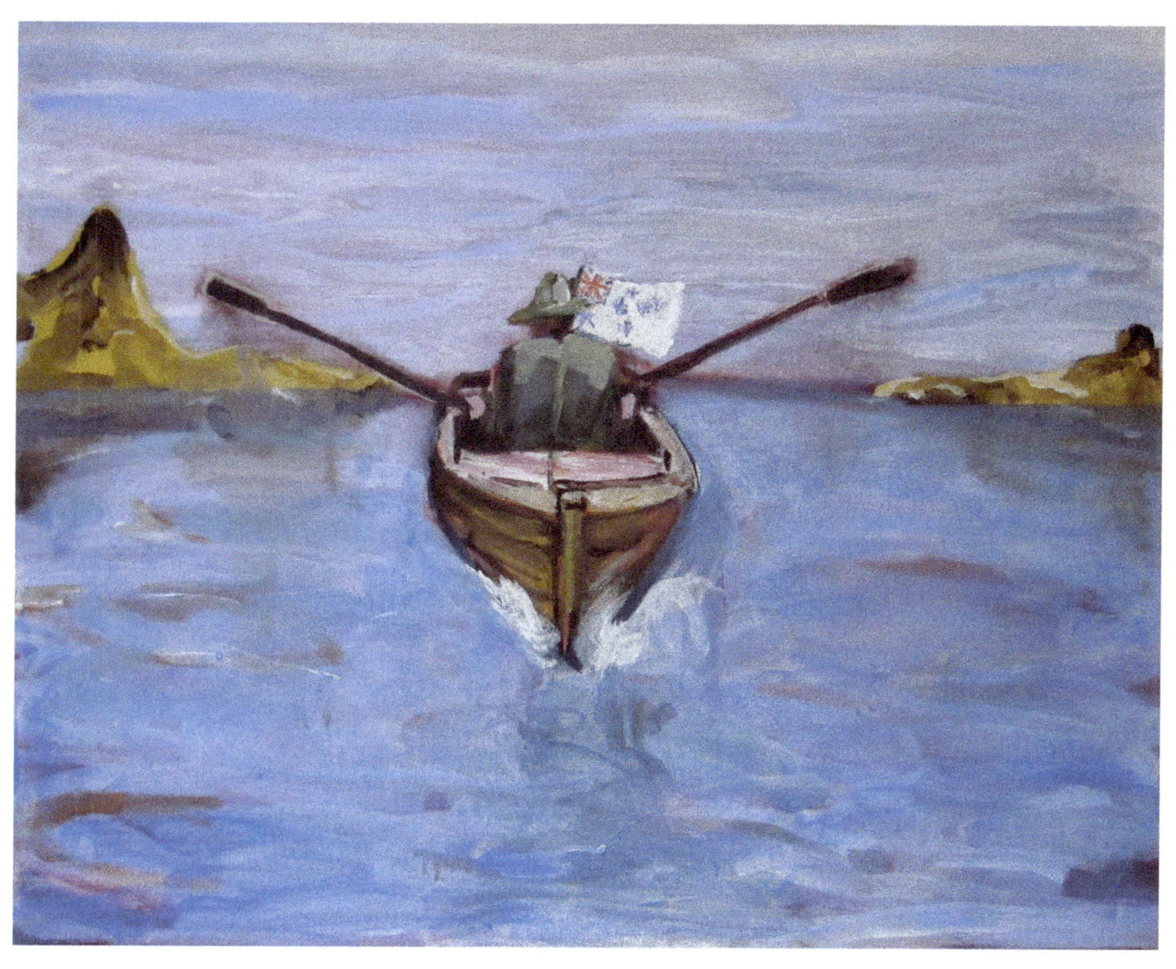

Setting up Supply Lines from the Ships
41 x 51 cm
acrylic on canvas board

...Chaplain Maitland-Woods is a decent old sort. He is quite mad, thoughly mad on old buried cities, and ancient peoples. Whenever the padre gets a chance, he climbs one of these big old mounds and a crowd congregates, Aussies and En Zeds, Tommies and Cameleers and Artillerists and heavens knows what not, while he holds forth and tells us that the Bedouins were the cut-throat Amalakites who harried David and were just as dirty a crowd thousands of years ago as they are to-day. Then the padre points up this very wadi and tells us of the queer old armies that struggled along it, tough old chaps who tended their flocks and annexed those of their neighbours - who skinned one another alive at times - who built cities that other people razed to the ground. Quaint people who lived and loved and fought and died and vanished within the very dust upon which we lie night after night. So, old diary, if I slug some pages from the past into you, don't be put out, for daily I am breathing these old chaps' dust into me.

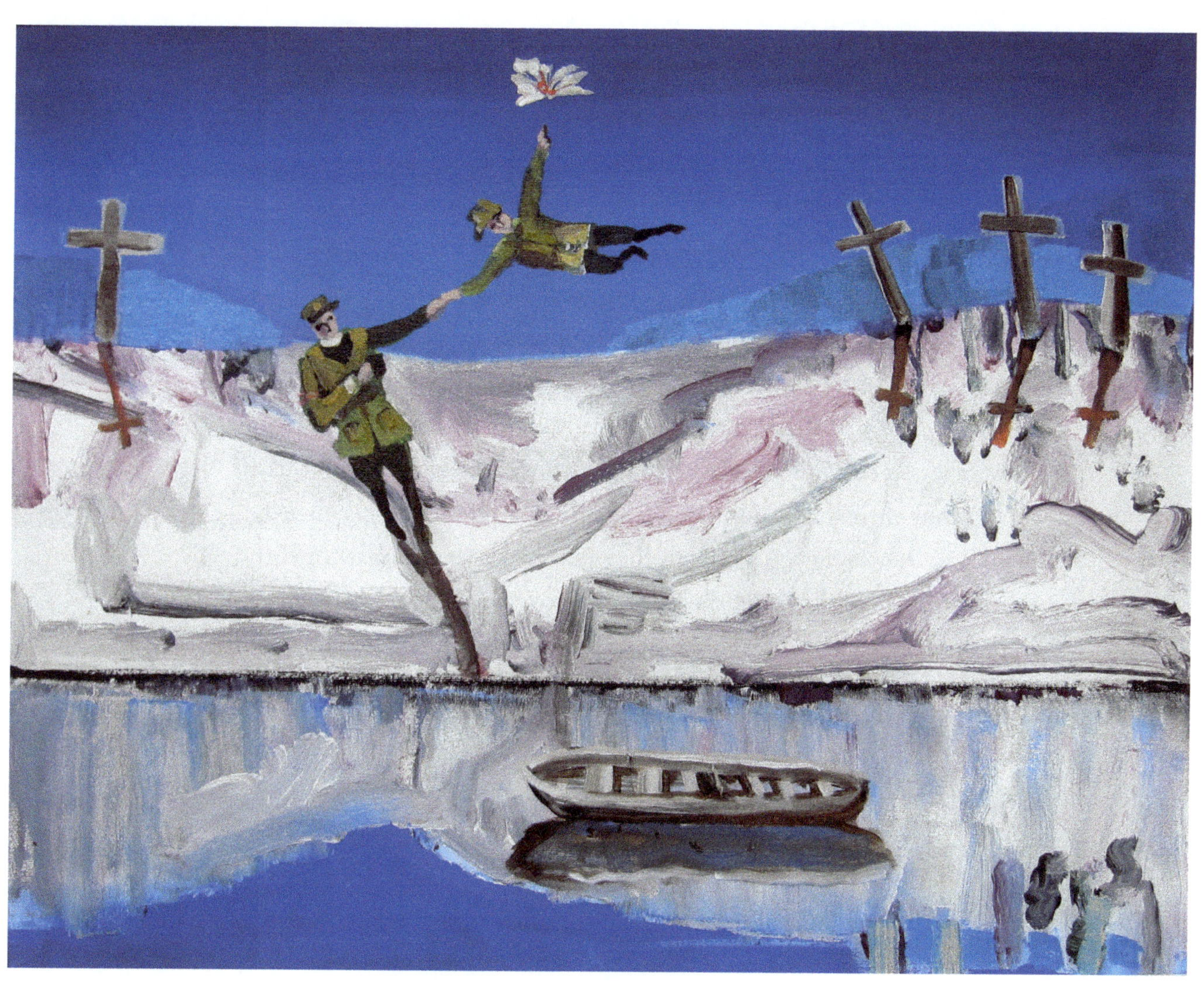

Chaplain Walter Bexter
41 x 51 cm
acrylic on canvas board

We climbed up the steep hill path, joking with the toil stained warriors who were cooking their evening meal, or toiling at the ammunition boxes, or lying like tired brown men about their tiny dugouts. Then we filed through a trench that led to the back of the hill and came out in a gloomy, narrow valley all tortuous and fissured as it wound through a sort of basin at the bottom of the big, sombre hills. We now faced many hills gutted with gorges, overshadowed a mile farther ahead by a flat rampart of cliffy peaks. An occasional shrapnel-shell screamed overhead. The whizz, zip, zip, zip of bullets became definite and unfriendly.

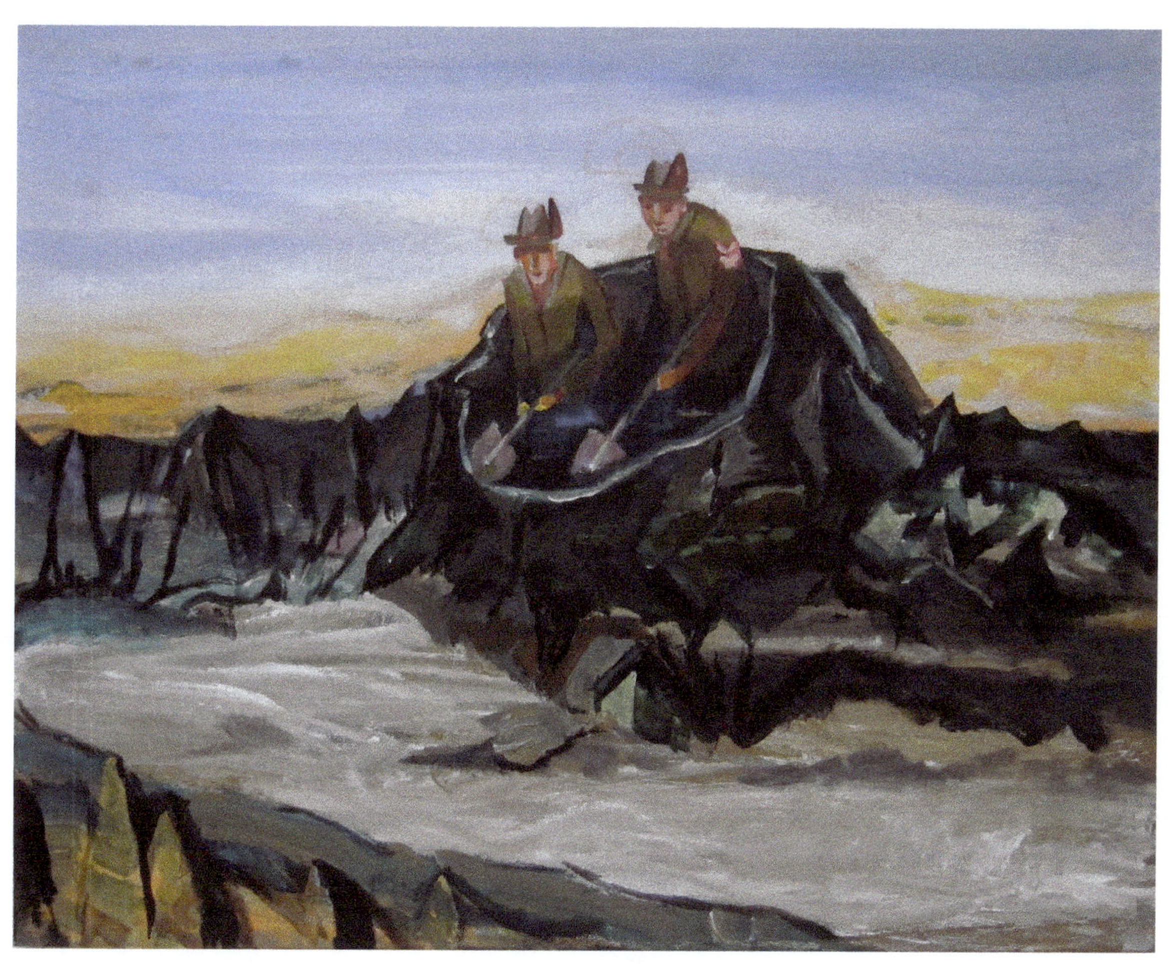

Stalemate - digging in
41 x 51 cm
acrylic on canvas board

At the Landing he commandeered a donkey and ever since has been coming and going from the distant firing-line to the beach with wounded men. He worked day and night, plodding along unscathed under fire till all thought he must be protected by supernatural means. His colonel long ago told him to carry on all on his own; to do whatever he liked and go wherever he liked.

He has been a little army of mercy all on his own.

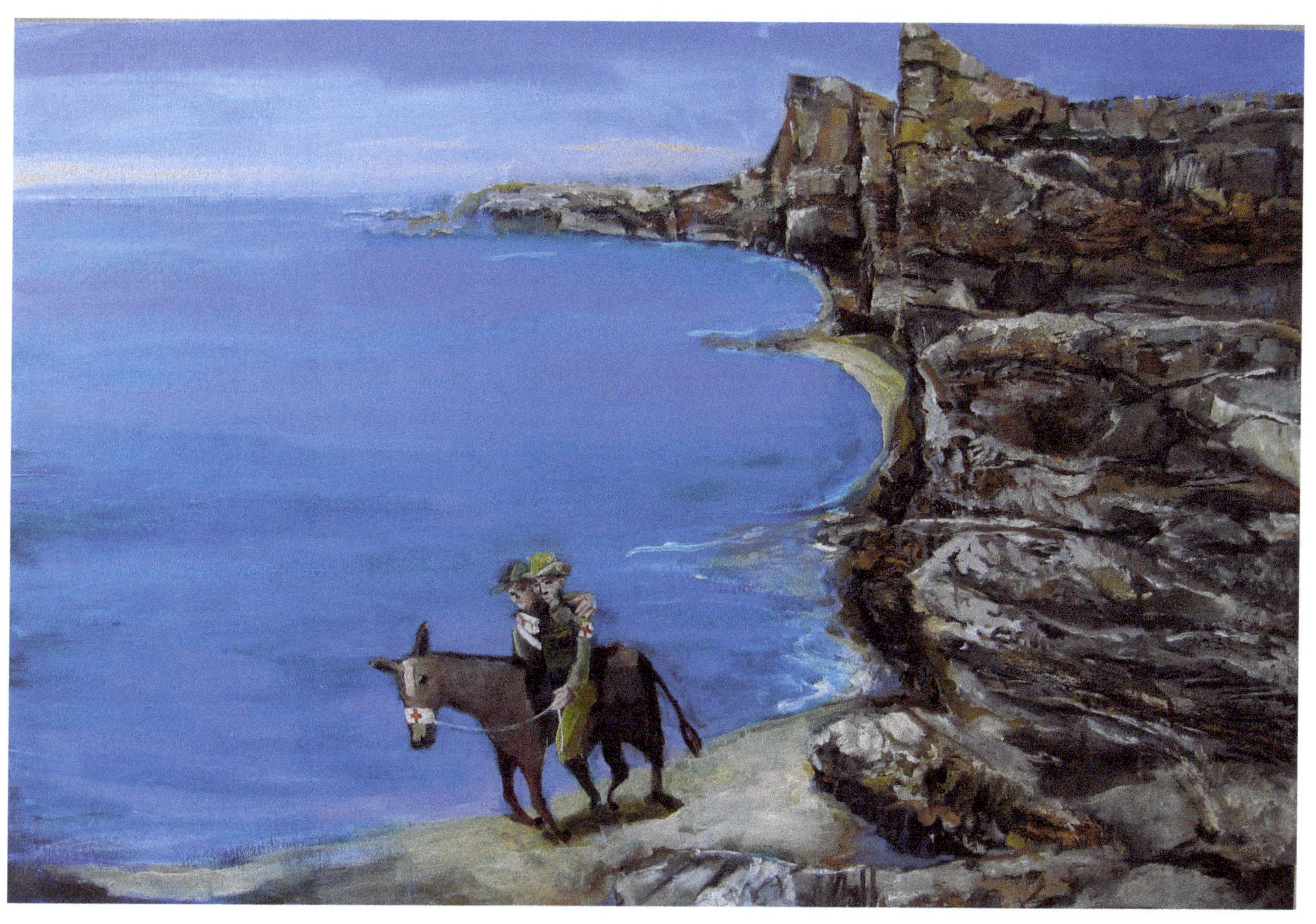

Simpson on the Beach
80 x 110 cm
acrylic on board

The infantry are quite cut up—not over their terrible losses, but
because of one man, Simpson Kirkpatrick I think his name is.
He was known everywhere as "Murph. and his Donk." ...
Yesterday morning, I think it was, he went up the valley and stopped by
the Water Guard where he generally had breakfast. It wasn't ready so he
went on, calling, "Never mind, give me a good dinner when I come back."

He never came back. Coming along the valley holding two wounded men
to the donkey he was shot through the heart. Both wounded men were
wounded again.

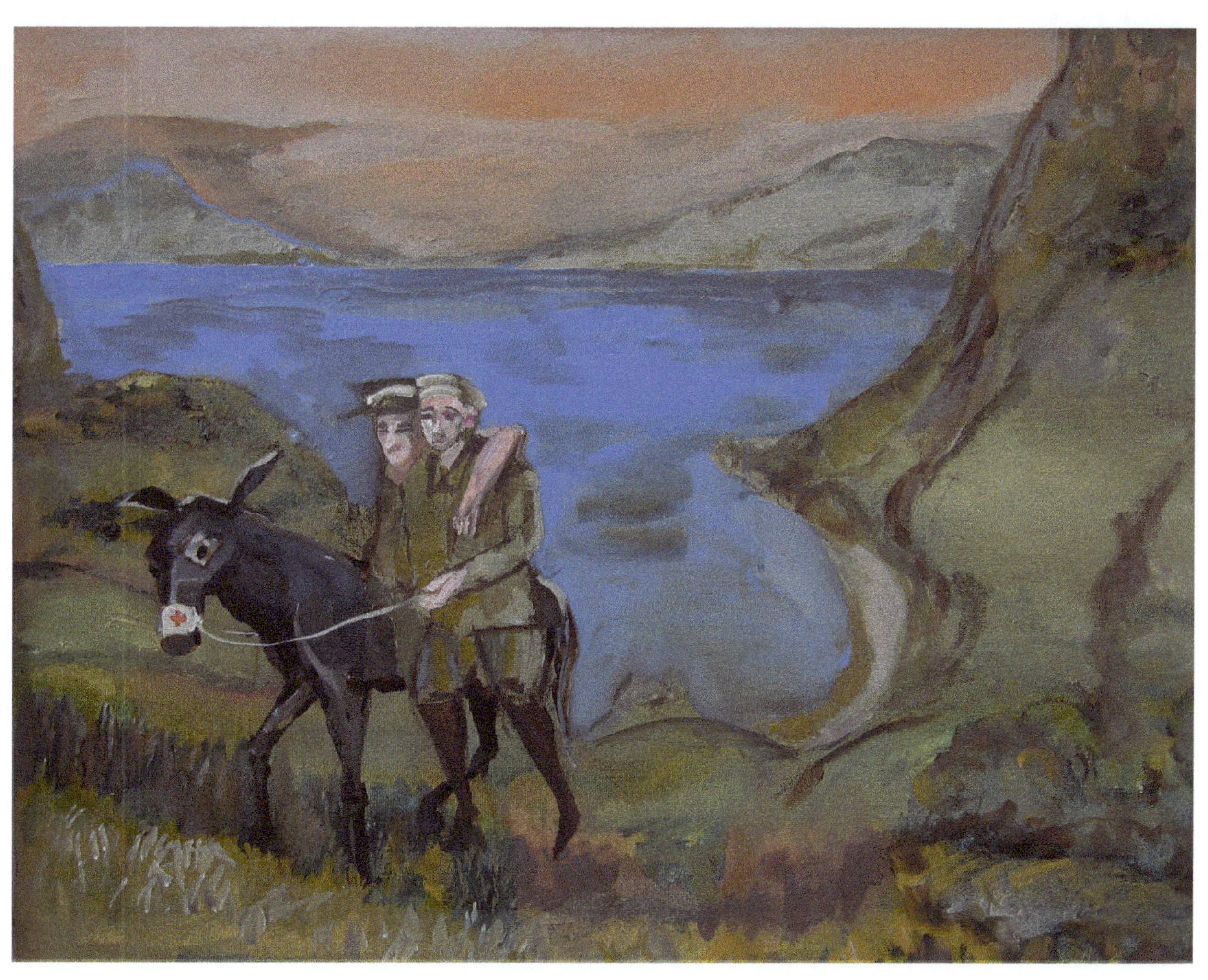

John Simpson Kirkpatrick & his donkey
41 x 51 cm
acrylic on canvas board

We went for a swim this evening. As the Turks sent an occasional shrapnel screaming across the wee beach, our bathing was in running dips. The beach is strewn with discarded equipment, broken rifles, numerous mess-tins, and water-bottles, all with shrapnel holes through them, lengths of barbed wire, jagged stakes, torn haversacks, and now and again a trampled-on felt hat with the little hole and black blood patch.

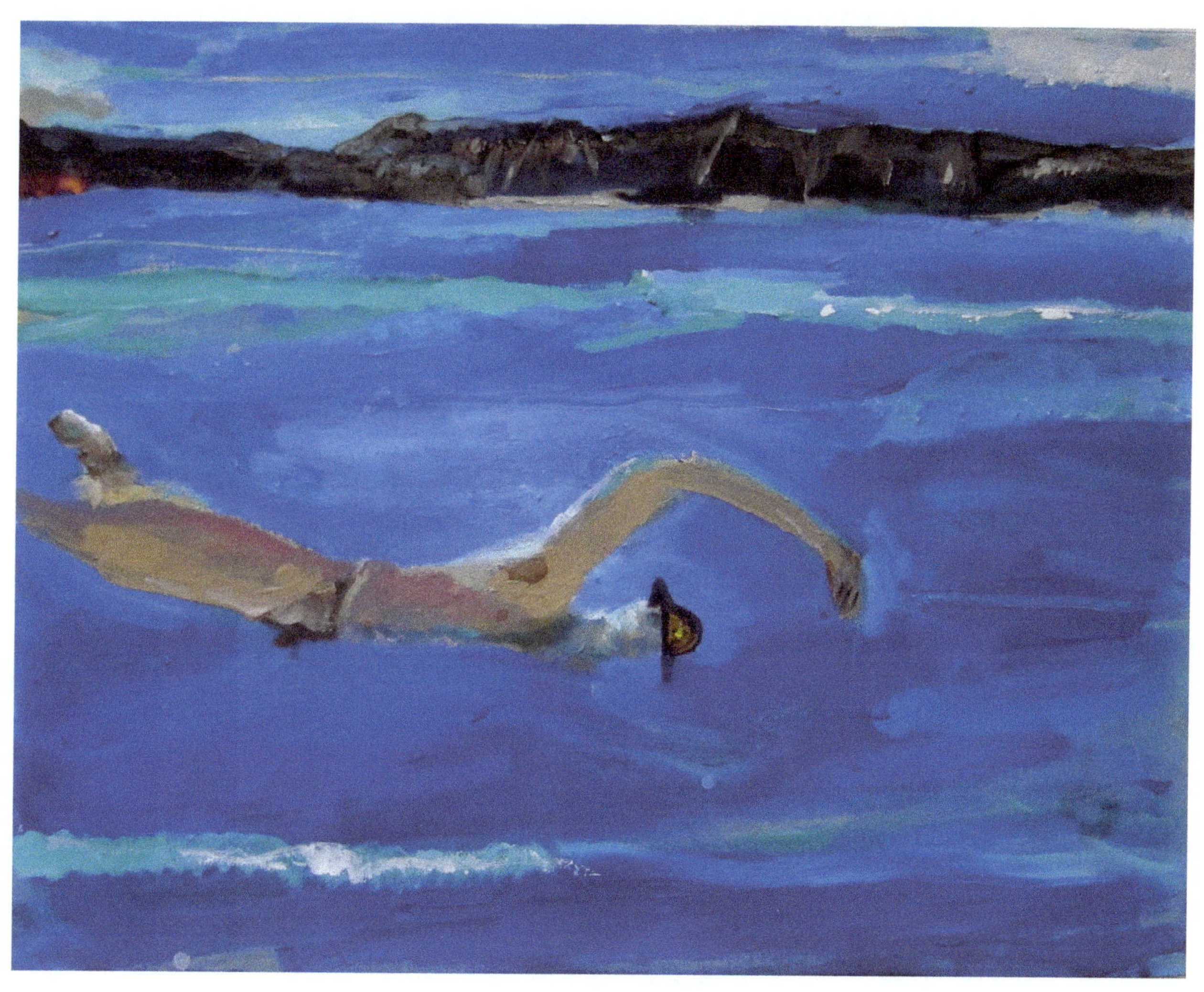

Soldier Swimming
41 x 51 cm
acrylic on canvas board

We worked in a sweating hurry as the night's inferno began, thankful that the tall hills sheltered us greatly from artillery-fire. But there came a rain of vicious bullets. One smacked a clod of earth down my neck and the old spine shivered to the grisly dirt. Heaven only knew what germs were in that soil from the battlefields of ages.

We belted into the digging again. A bullet sighed clean through Nix's hat. It rained bullets for a while and we crouched in our holes like anxious mice, wishing they were deeper.

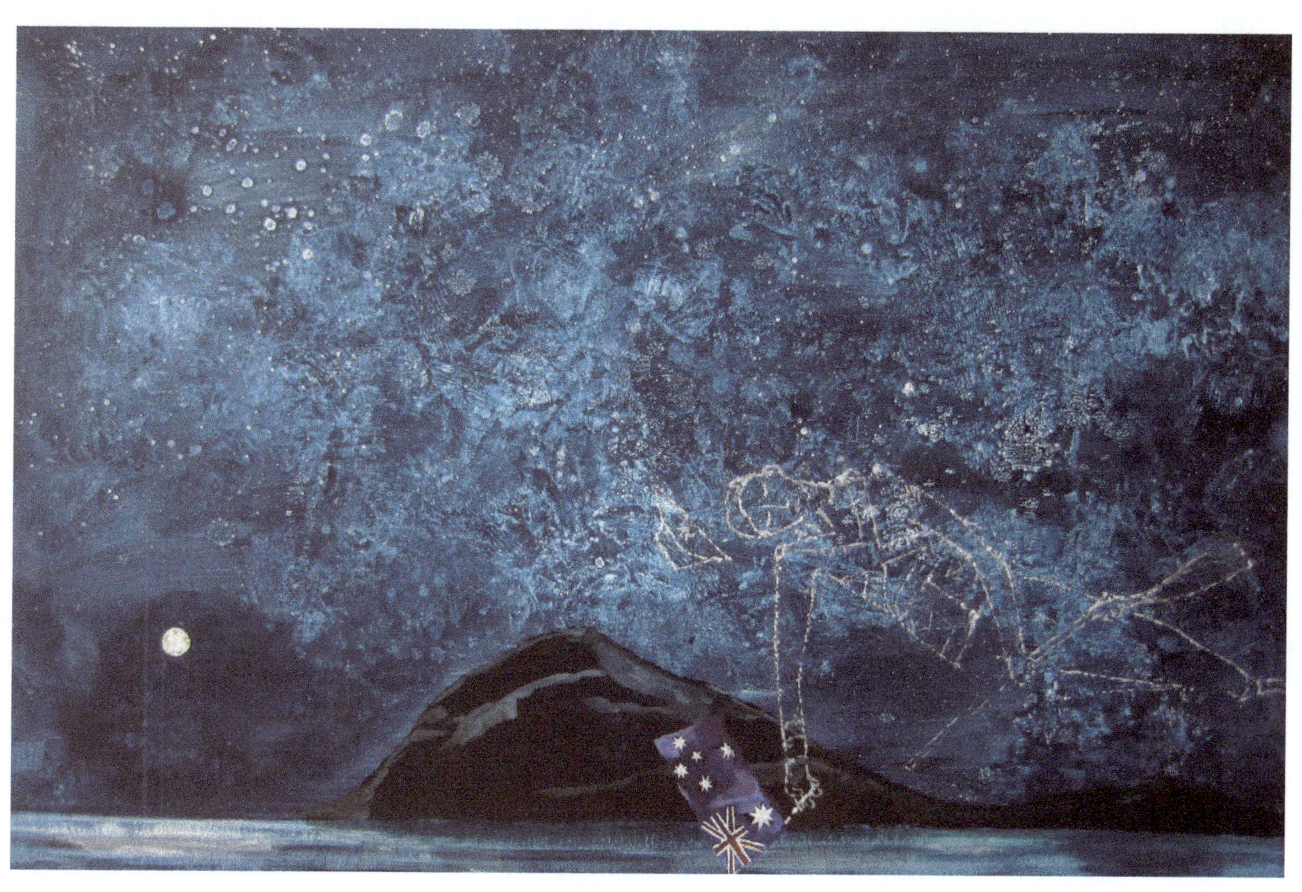

Under Foreign Skies
80 x 110 cm
acrylic on board

We went for a swim this evening. As the Turks sent an occasional shrapnel screaming across the wee beach, our bathing was in running dips. The beach is strewn with discarded equipment, broken rifles, numerous mess-tins, and water-bottles, all with shrapnel holes through them, lengths of barbed wire, jagged stakes, torn haversacks, and now and again a trampled-on felt hat with the little hole and black blood patch.

These are the relics of the landing of the first battalions and each tragic lot of flotsam tells its own story. I picked up a sand-dirtied photo of a woman and kiddy, with a bullet hole through it. The graves of the men line the beach, their shrapnel-torn boats lie overturned at the water's edge. It seems pitiful waste, men and everything smashed—and hearts in Australia too.

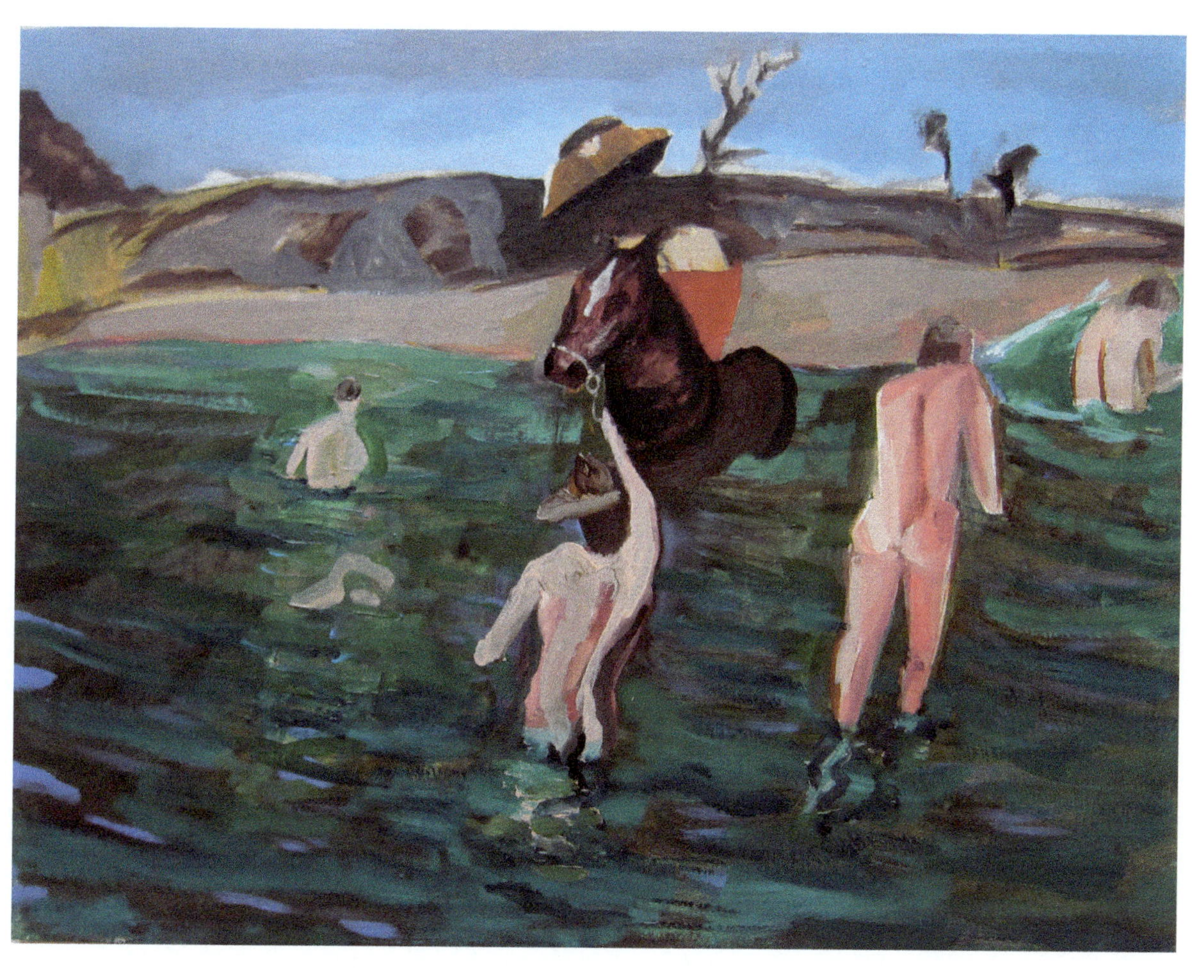

Bathing 1
41 x 51 cm
acrylic on canvas board

We went for a swim this evening... The night, away from the bases of the hills, was only semi-dark. The bullets coming so far were mostly high shots flying over the tops of our trenches which clung to the cliffy hills above.

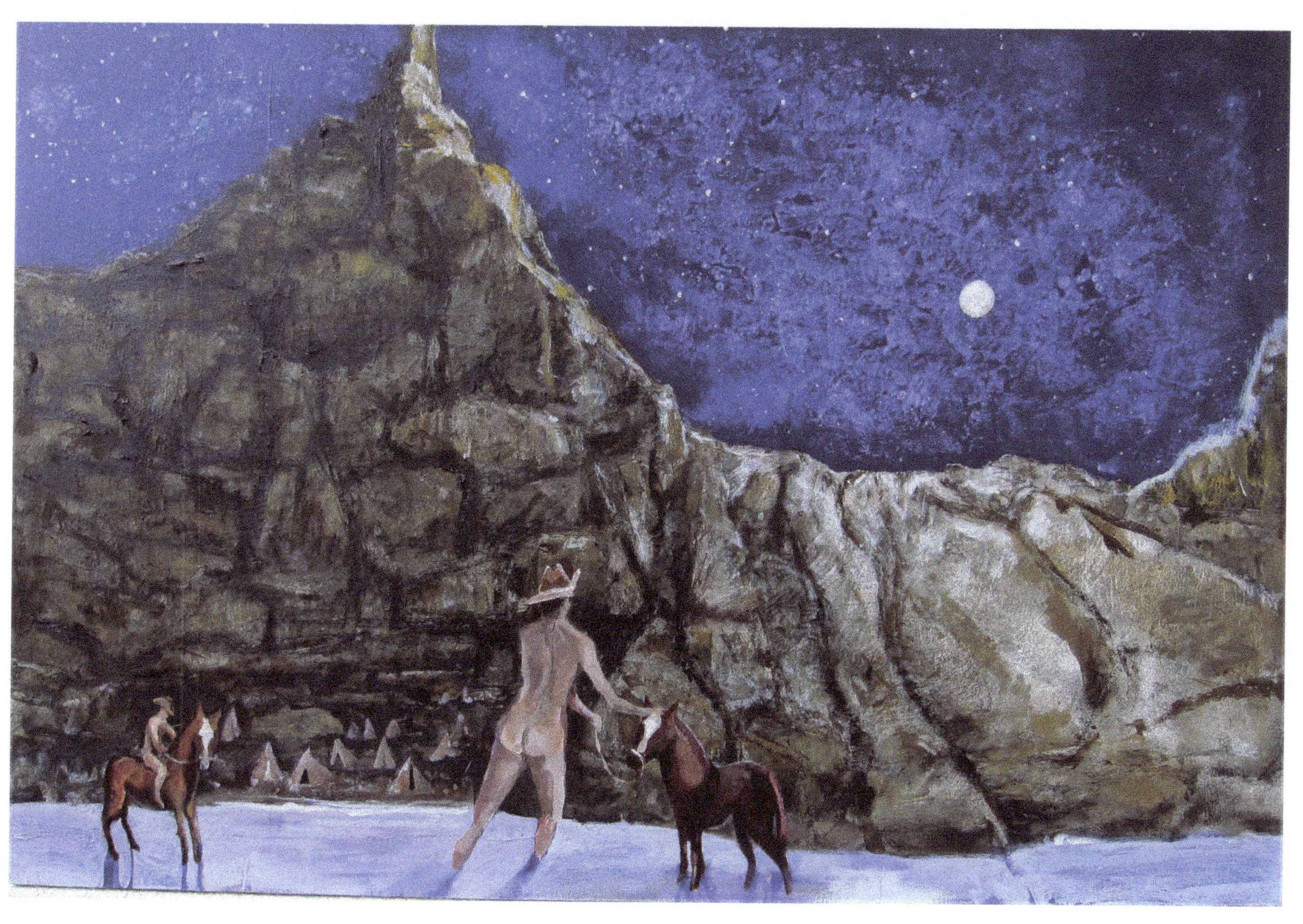

Bathing at Night
80 x 110 cm
acrylic on board

Our big howitzer is replying to the enemy's fire. She invariably does when the firing gets too hot for us. Of course, we are only one little group. There are other battalions and regiments for miles. They all have troubles of their own. So our howitzer looks after us and it is warmly cheering to hear that big shell tearing through the air overhead on its vengeful errand, and then the distant bang!—fair on the enemy's trenches, we hope, or better still, on some hidden gun.

We were bathing just now when a shell came and wounded McDonald and Liddell, both of my own troop. Bathing is off—until tomorrow.

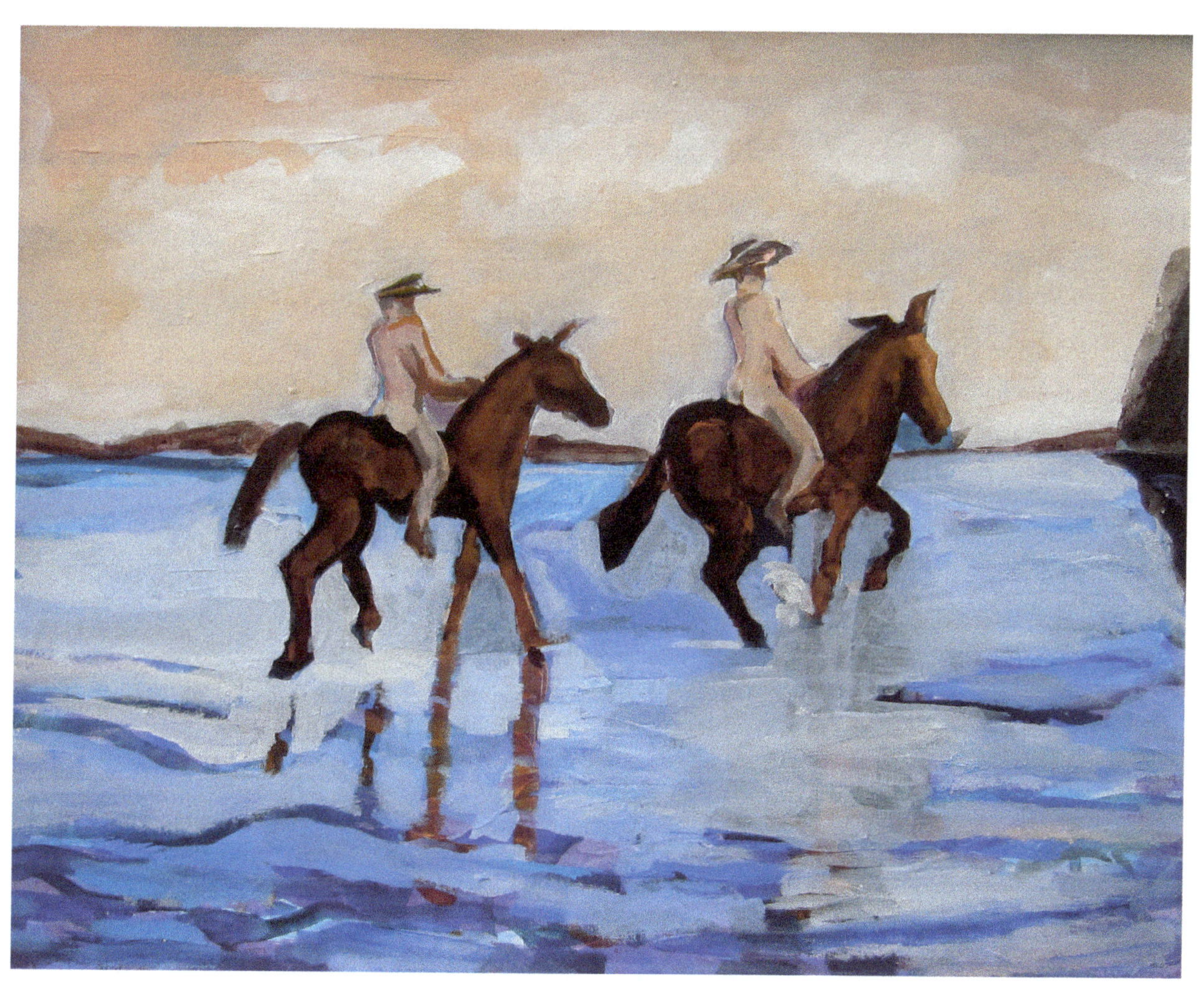

Bathing the Walers
41 x 51 cm
acrylic on canvas board

No doubt this is a real spell.
No idiotic stirrup polishing or such like tommy-rot.
Plenty of bathing, sleep, and fresh water.
Just enough training to keep us fit.

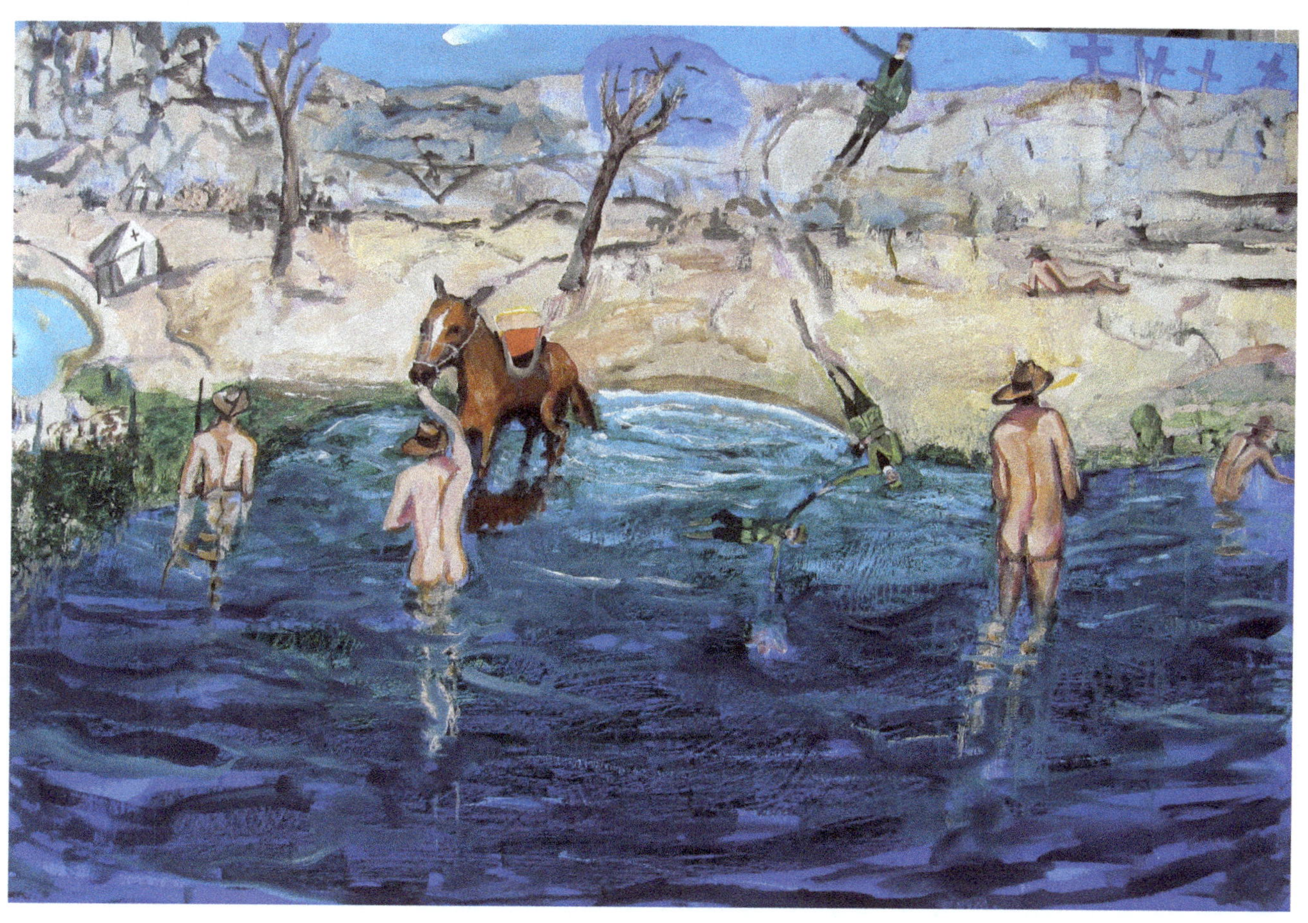

Bathing the Blessing
80 x 110 cm
acrylic on board

Surf-bathing this afternoon, Surf-bathing!
It's a wonder the sea did not take a fit …

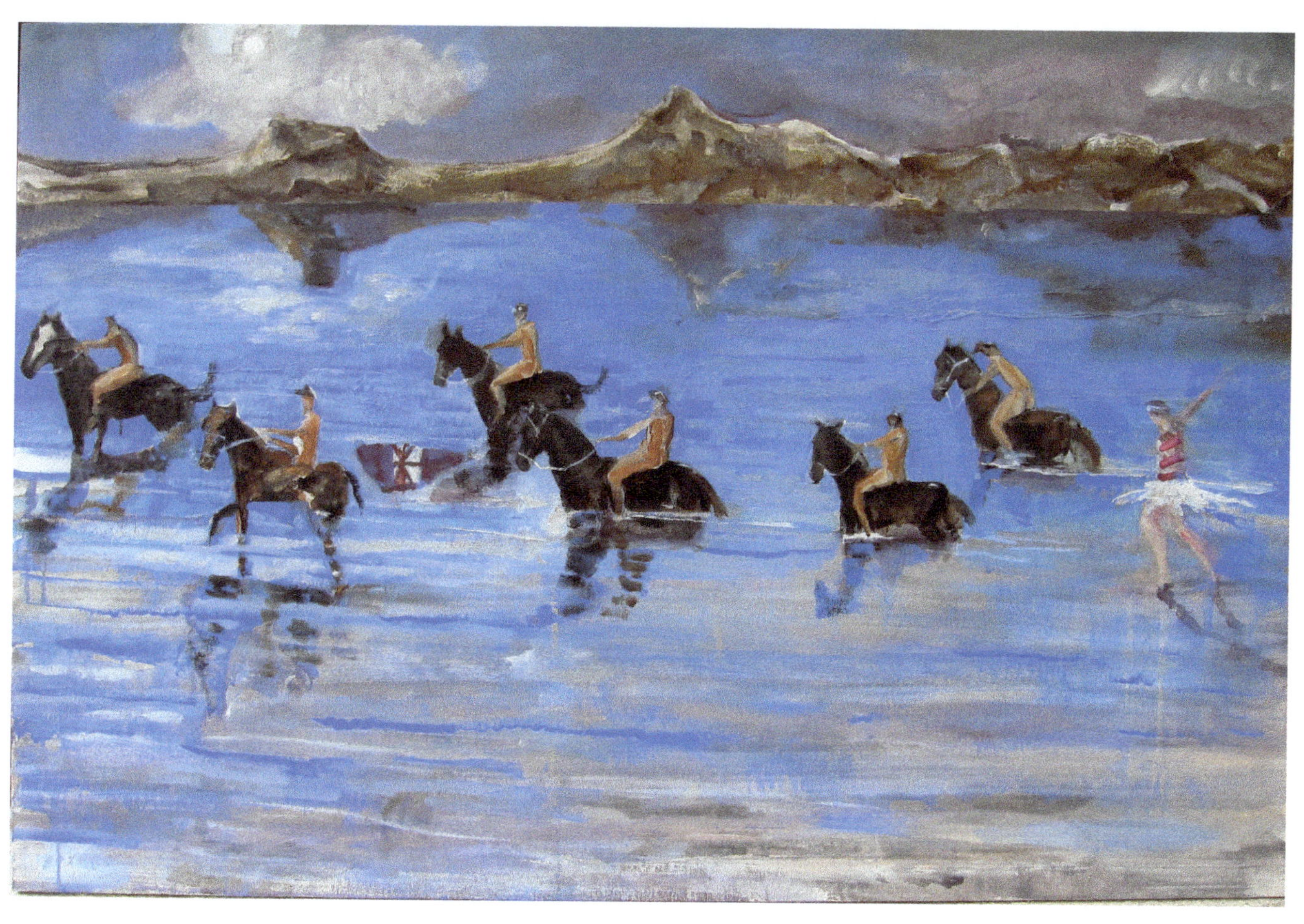

Bathing Dancing
80 x 110 cm
acrylic on board

Presently we crept in again, and anchored and went while the going was good. Were jolly glad to step on shore among huge stacks of ammunition and stores. Men were bathing—so strange it seemed that men were dying too. Men were toiling among the heavy stacks of stores, men trudged all over that tiny beach in ragged, clay-stained uniforms, their familiar Australian faces cheerful and grimy under sprouting beards.

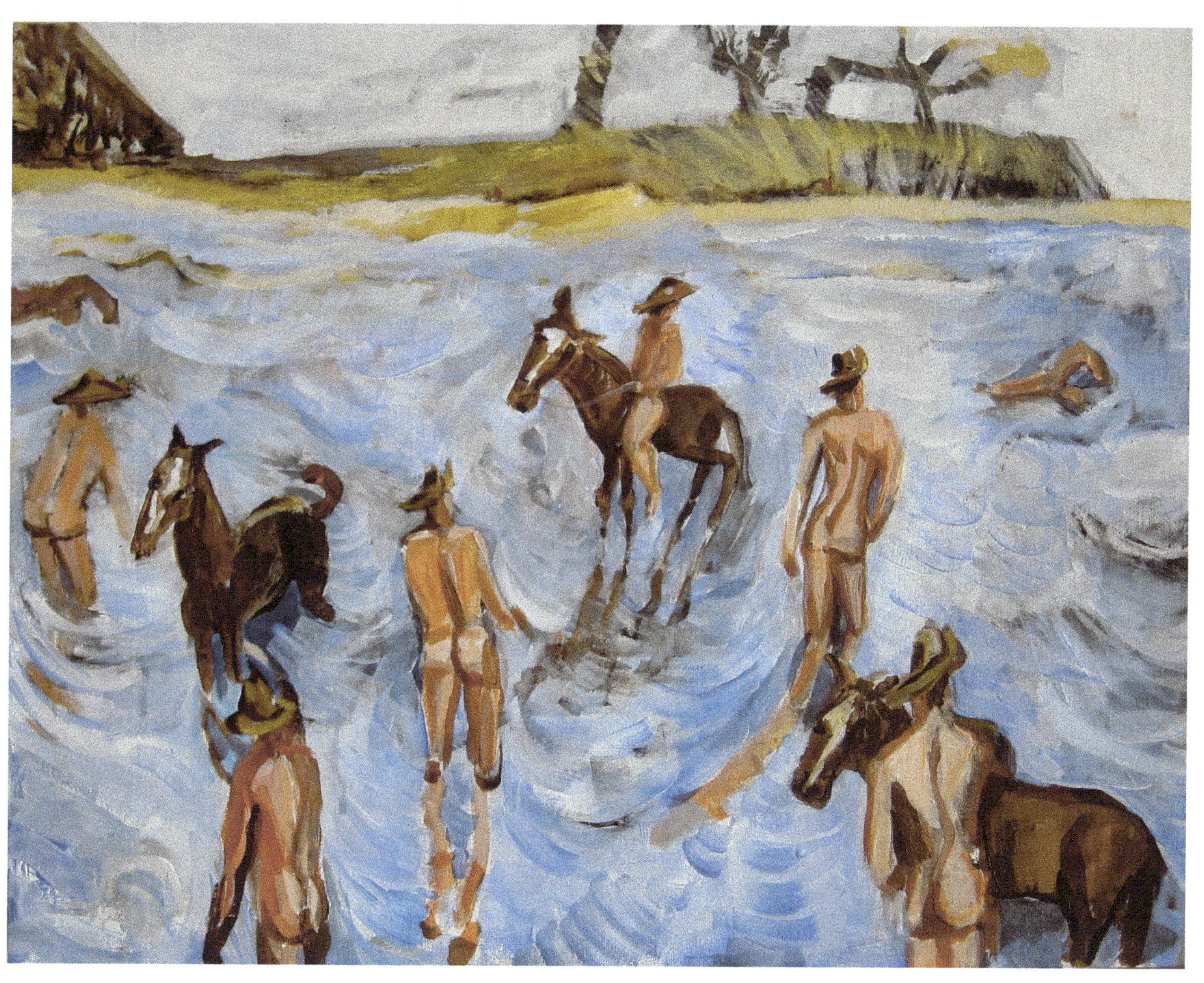

Bathing
41 x 51 cm
acrylic on canvas board

June 21st—Yesterday, fifteen bags of mail (thousands of letters) came for the 5th. And yet there was not one solitary letter, parcel, or even newspaper for me.

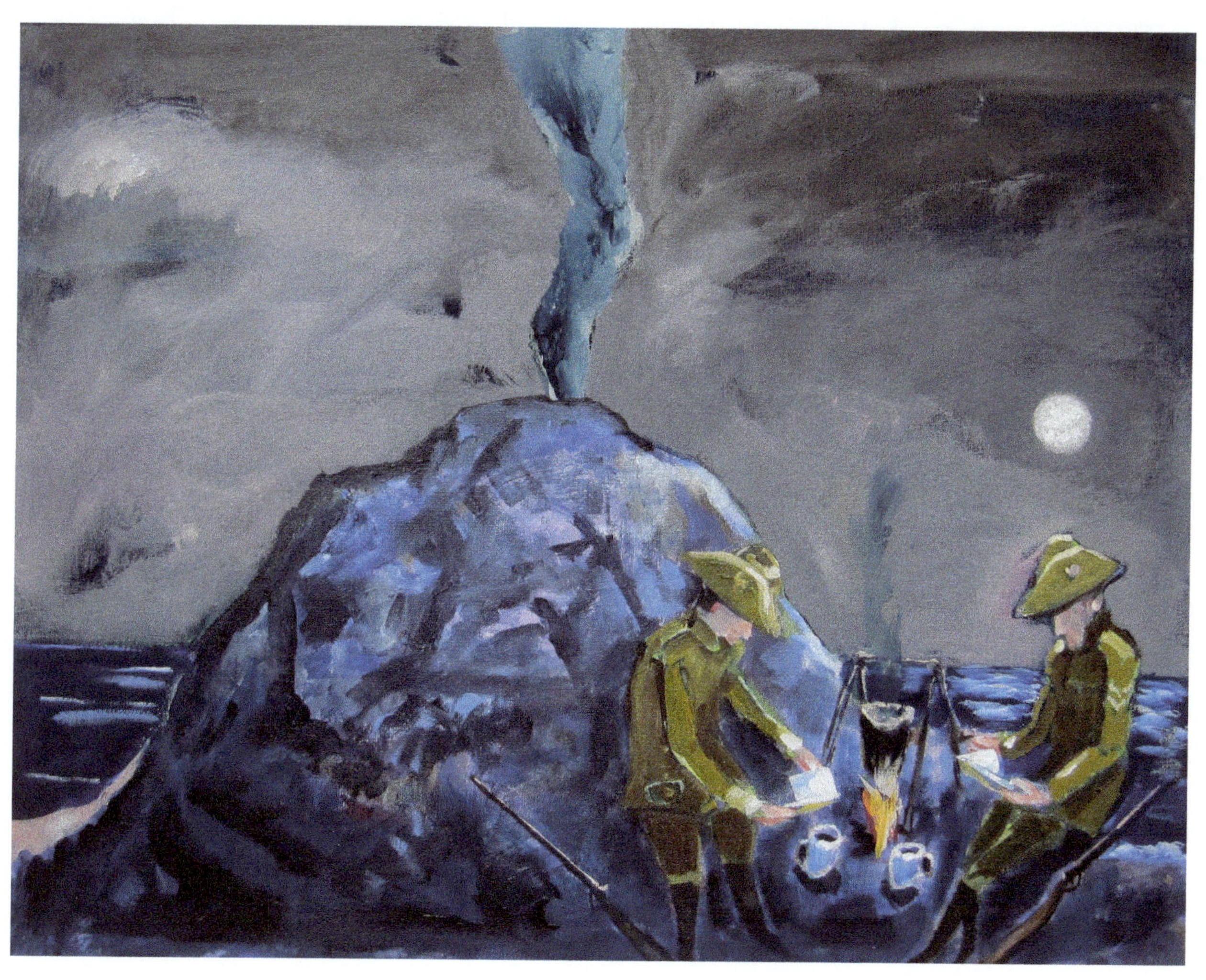

Letters from Home
41 x 51 cm
acrylic on canvas board

…We've been issued with the blasted hard old biscuits again The boys are just wild to have a go at old Jacko in the open. We know that he is the equal of any soldiers in the world at trench and bomb fighting, but there is a spirit of utter confidence among all of us that we are individually better men. We will soon know.

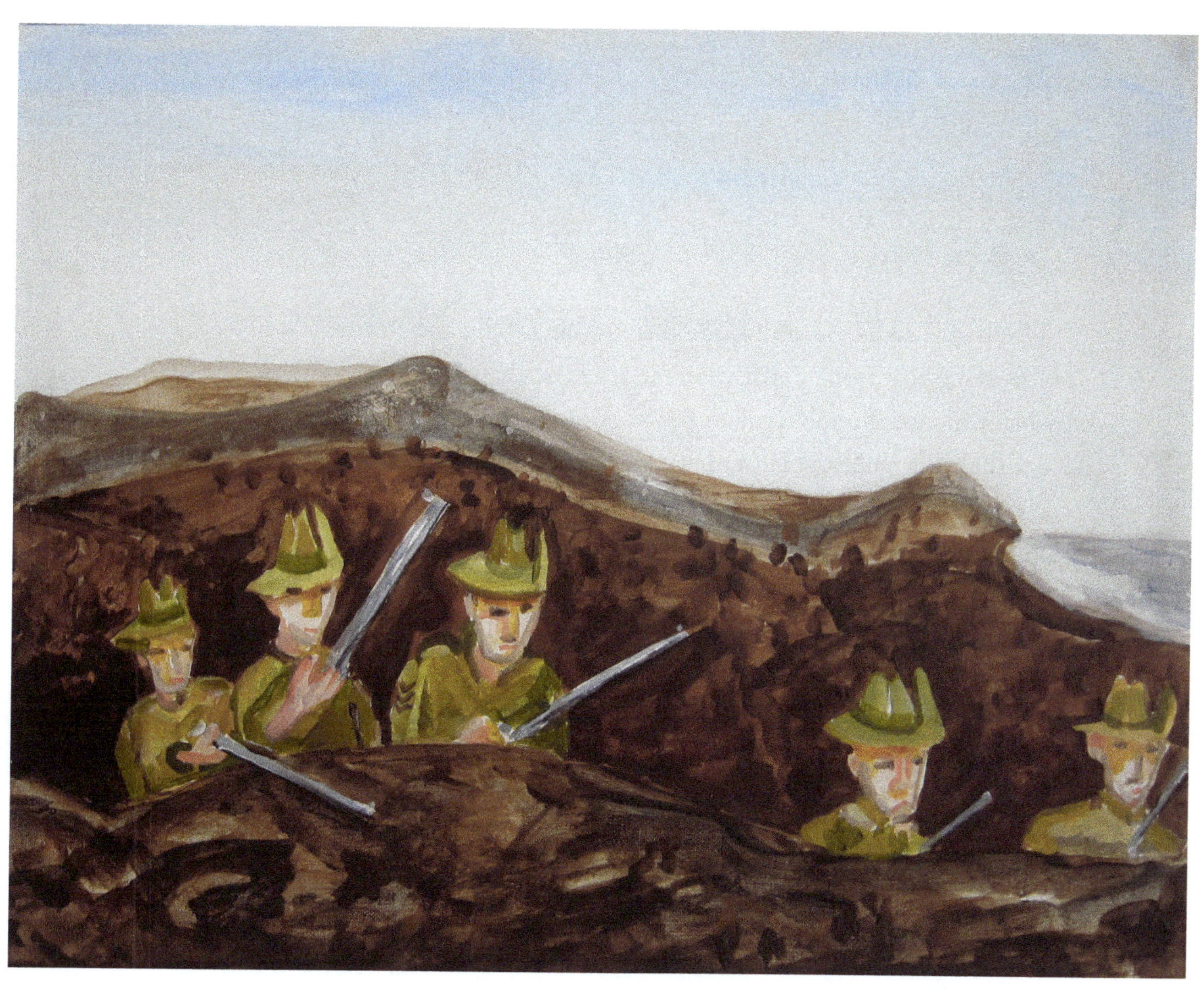

In the Trench
41 x 51 cm
acrylic on canvas board

…I "spotted" awhile for Billy Sing this morning. Billy and I came down on the same boat from Townsville. He is a little chap, very dark, with a jet-black moustache and a goatee beard. A picturesque looking man killer. He is the crack sniper of the Anzacs. His tiny possy is perched in a commanding position high up in the trench. He does nothing but sniping. He has already shot one hundred and five Turks. He has a splendid telescope and through it I peered across at a distant loophole, just in time to see a Turkish face framed behind the loophole. He disappeared. A few minutes later, and part of his face appeared. That vanished… Then he showed all his face and disappeared.
He didn't reappear again, though I kept turning the telescope back to his possy. At last, farther along the line, I spotted a man's face framed enquiringly in a loophole. He stayed there. Billy fired. The Turk vanished instantly, but with the telescope I could partly see the motion of men inside the trench picking him up.

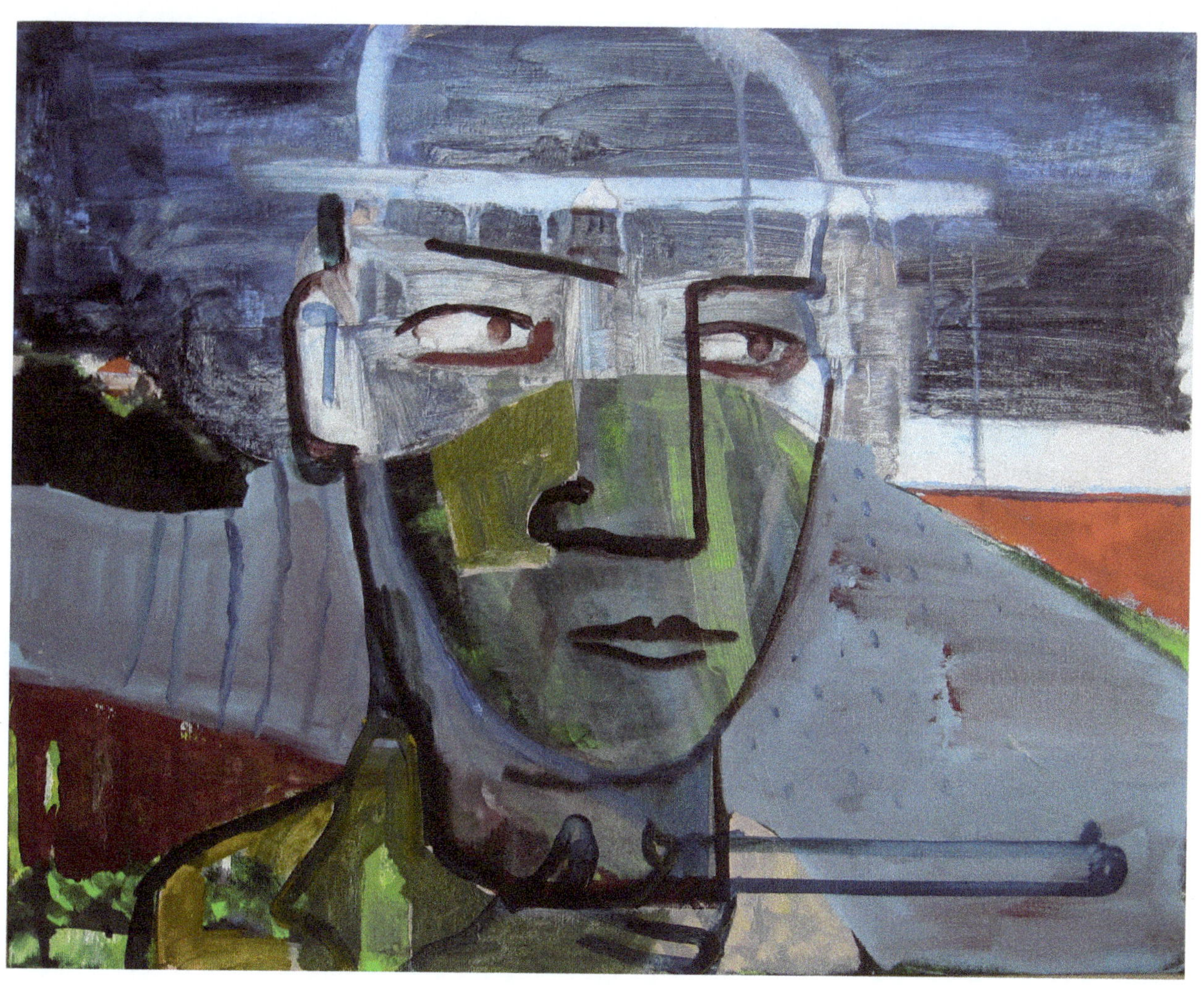

Sniper
41 x 51 cm
acrylic on canvas board

Every one helped each other in this dreadful ordeal.

It is getting fearfully hot now, shells are exploding every few seconds; the row is an inferno made hellish by the hot smell of fumes.

The cry is becoming continuous, "Stretcher-bearers!" "Stretcher-bearers!" "Doctor!" as more and more of our poor chaps get hit. Good luck to all the medical men! We have the shelter of our dugouts, but they run out into this hail of shrapnel directly the cry goes up. The pity of it is that we cannot fire a shot in return.

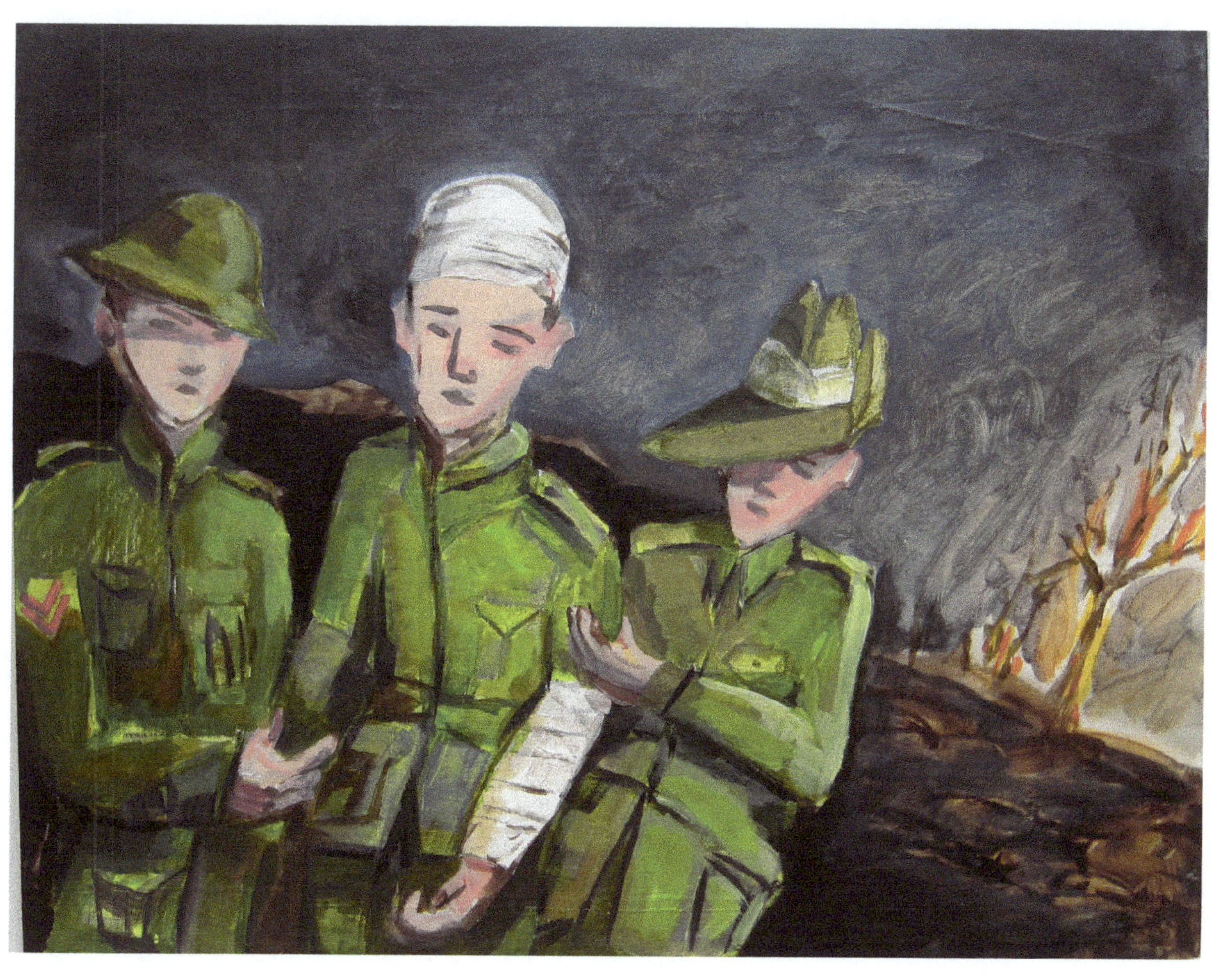

Wounded Soldier
41 x 51 cm
acrylic on canvas board

Well, the dark came, bringing a vicious increase of rifle-fire. The top layer of our possy was only one sandbag thick. The bullets ripped into this, and the sand began to flow out. As the top layer of bags subsided we had to crouch lower, otherwise our heads would have been blown off. Then came one continuous screech of bullets, a piercing chorus, ceaseless throughout the night. Then the roar of bombs in earnest, exploding in front of our trench, around us, behind us, with a blinding flash and roar! and clouds of earth and smoke, and the stench of burning cloth. Soon my mate and I had to smash two apertures through our parapet so that we could peer through and shoot the shadowy bombing men. What hell was let loose outside and all around us!

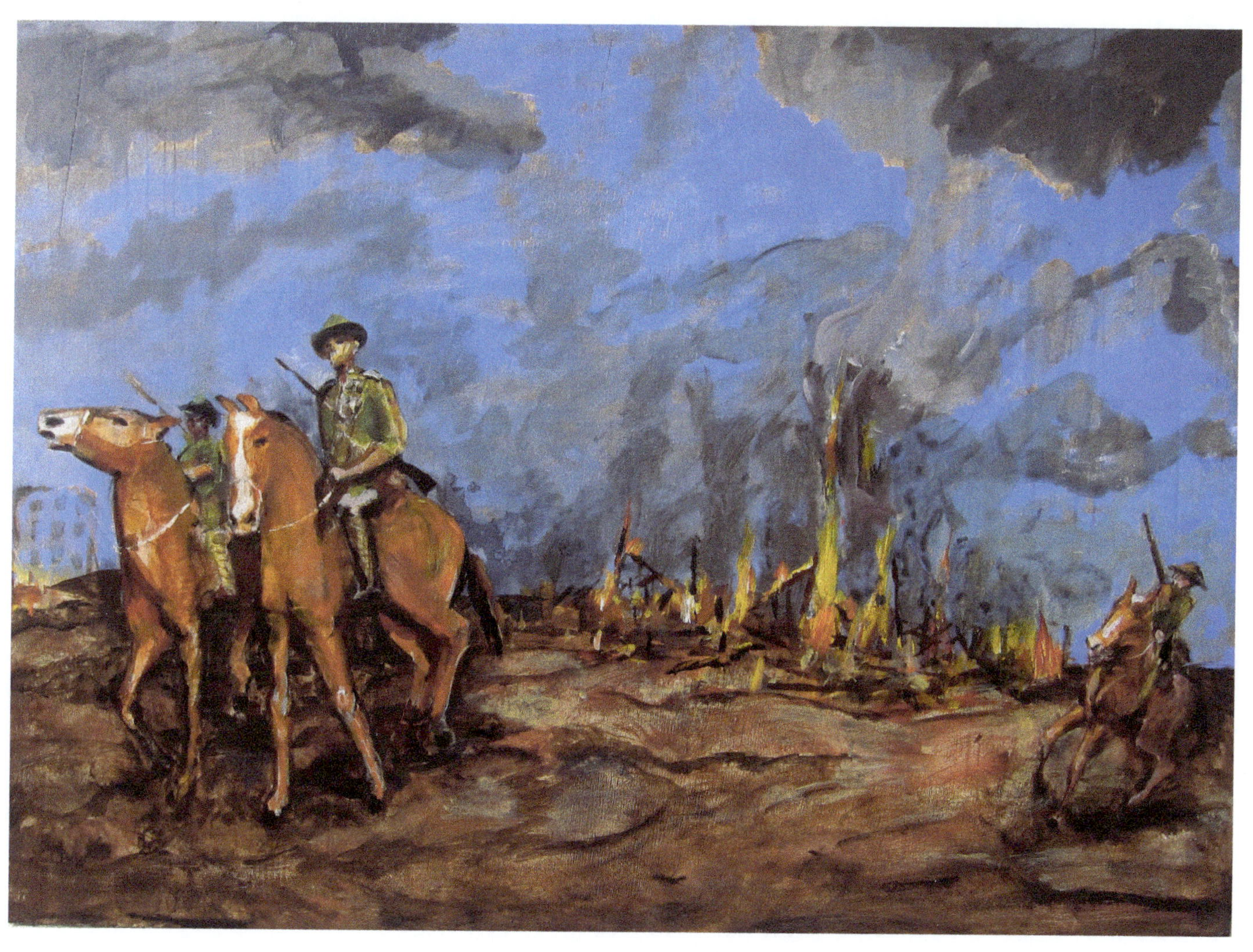

Smoke & fire
80 x 110 cm
acrylic on board

This time we galloped off from under the roaring muzzles of our own guns. The horses got excited, we got excited, we leant over their necks and shouted and laughed in a mad exhilaration. The Turks could see us and they hurled over the shrapnel until the very air seemed one long scream all rent with bursting shells. The bullets hummed faster, our own guns roared faster, the horses galloped faster, and out in front of the regiment, his tail mast-high, head erect, neighing frantically, there raced wildly excited a long, bony horse which had been hard hit and should have been dead an hour ago.
He was having the last grand gallop of his life.

So we thundered to cover again but the wounded horse raced straight up on to the skyline where he pranced in a circle, neighing the regiment to come on until abruptly he dropped.

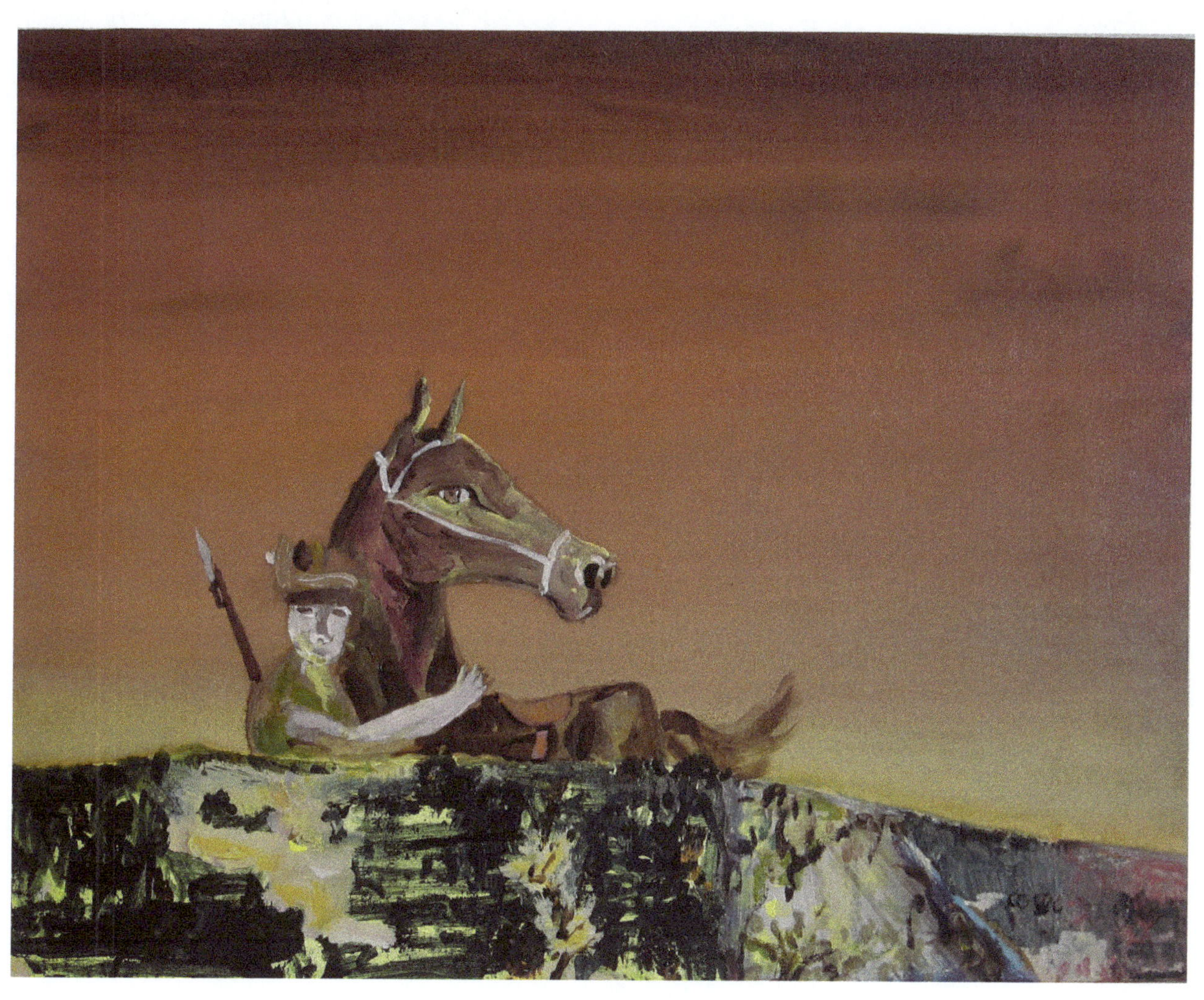

Wounded Horse
41 x 51 cm
acrylic on canvas board

The minesweeper is standing by. We are re-embarking for the final four hours' trip. There was a storm at sea last night. This morning driving rain and mist temporarily blot out the shipping. The rough sea looks cold. We hope it. is not raining on the Peninsula for the cold there is intense. We old hands are just taking things as they come.

Whatever happens, must happen. That is the best way, after all.
We have all our equipment ready. The pack of the Light Horseman on foot is heavy and clumsy. A man will do some slipping about if those Gallipoli hills are muddy.

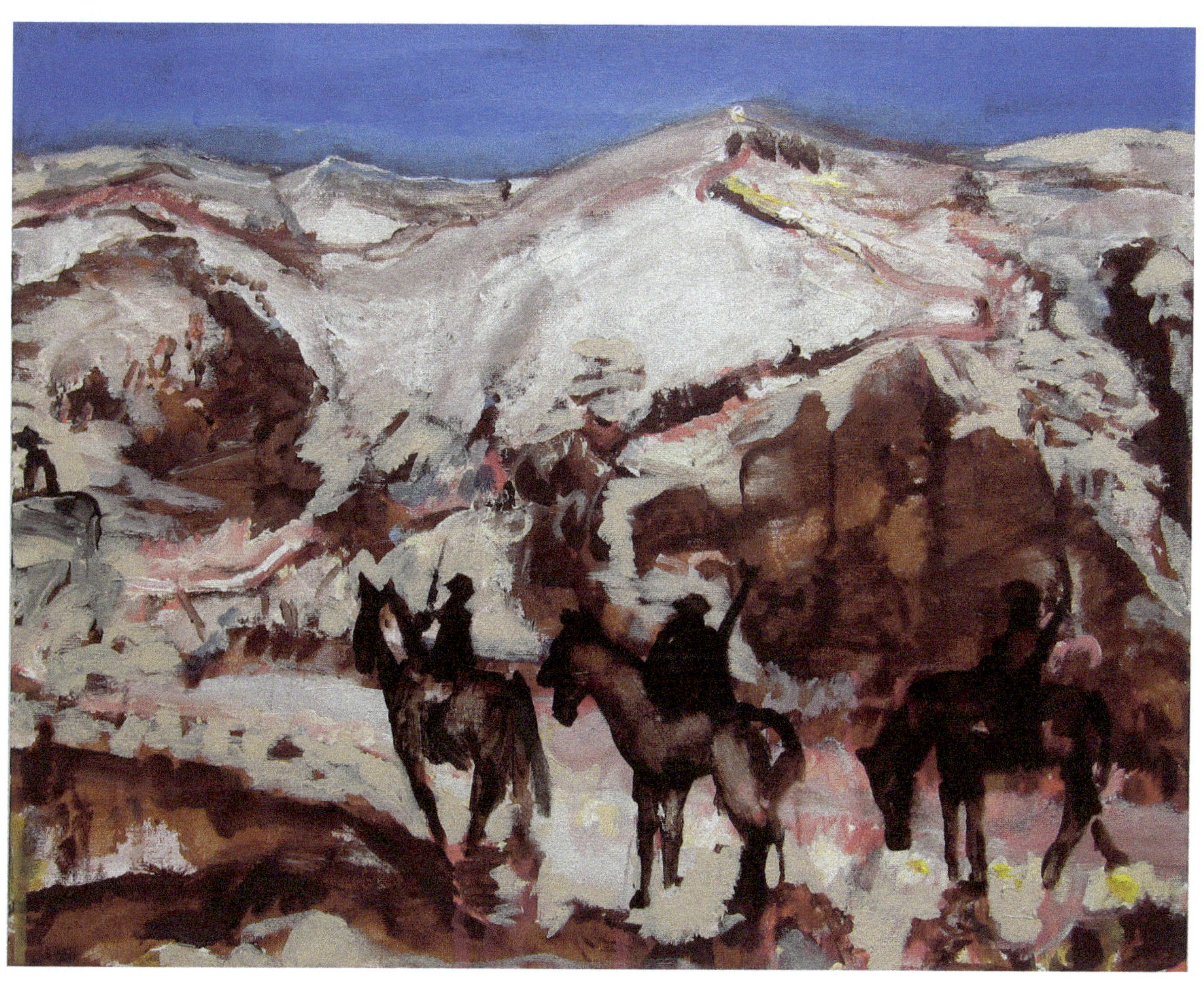

Winter Mission
41 x 51 cm
acrylic on canvas board

We sneaked into the Landing at ten o'clock last night. A hospital-ship was beautifully lighted on the still waters. Here and there fires gleamed on the old dark hills, and far down on the new Landing at Salt Lake. Those grim black hills waiting there seemed to spread a sinister atmosphere all over the bay. Desultory firing was going on with an odd sharp outburst of machine-gun fire at Salt Lake. All night long we were disembarking, only a few hundred men too, crouched shivering in those big iron barges. The steam pinnace took hours to tow the three barges the stone's throw to the shore.

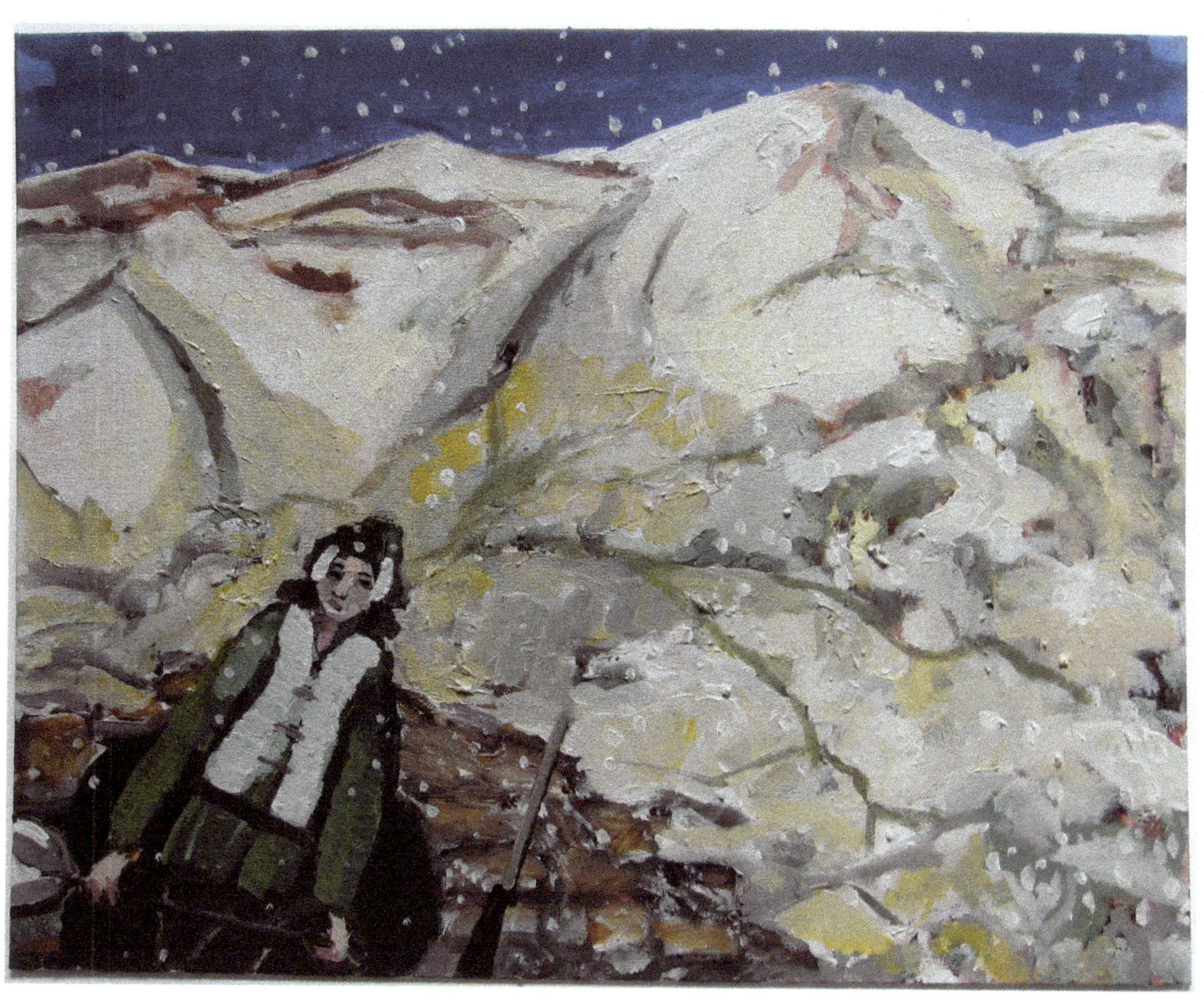

Enduring the Winter
41 x 51 cm
acrylic on canvas board

I felt awfully glad our casualties were practically nil. I pitied our odd unrecoverable dead lying away back. They must be very lonely.

Our wounded were in hell, but at long last they would reach a hospital and sleep, sleep, sleep!

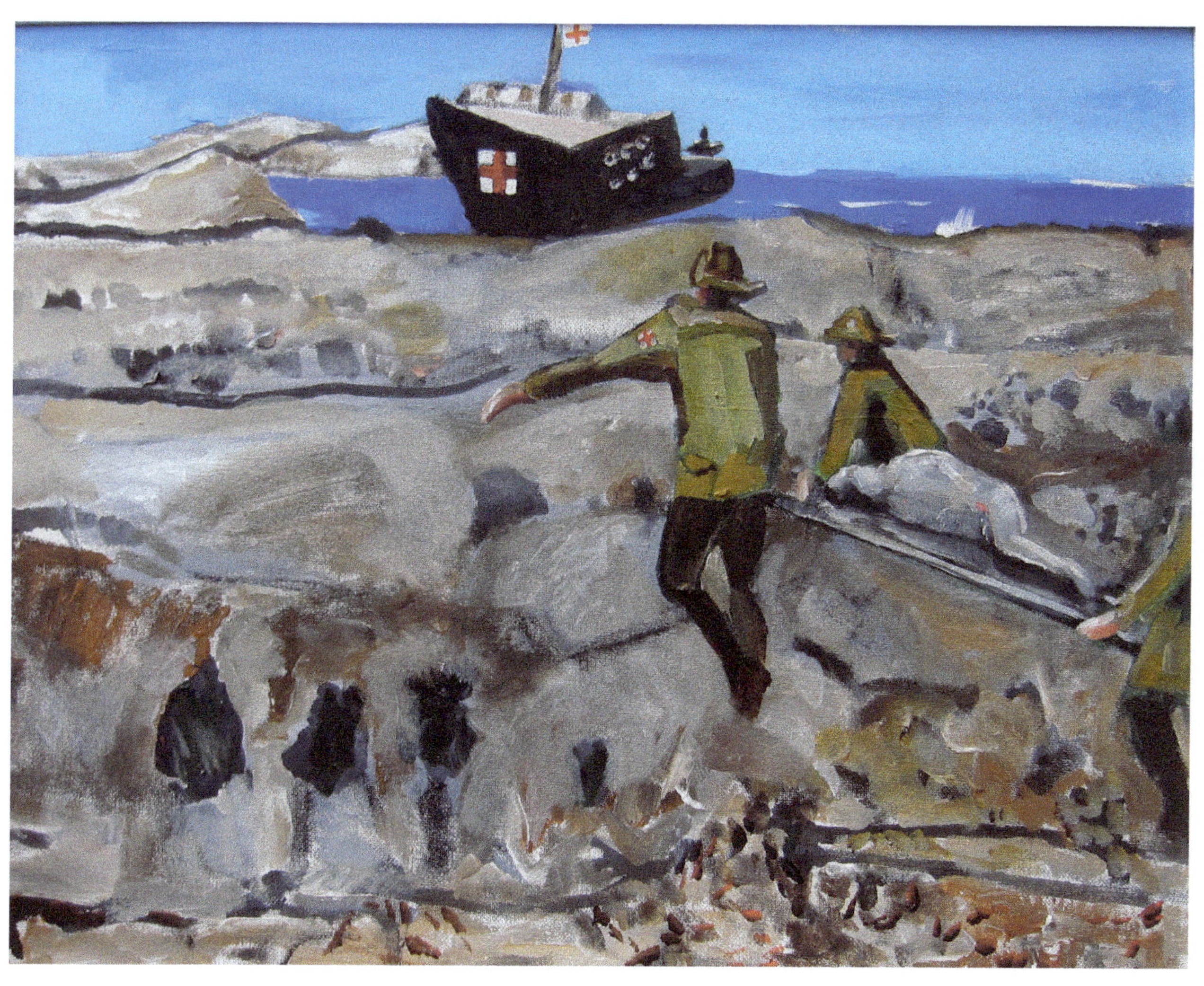

Wouded being Evacuated
41 x 51 cm
acrylic on canvas board

We moved off for the shore all ears to the pop, pop, pop of rifle-shots. Smoke fairly belched from the toy funnel: I suppose the sweating devils below were shoving the coal into her.

Nothing happened until we got closer inshore and the bushes on the hillsides began to take shape. Then whizzz, then ping, ping, ping, ping. By jove, rifle-bullets! Whizz-zz, smack! and a shrill receding whistle as the bullet ricocheted off the water.

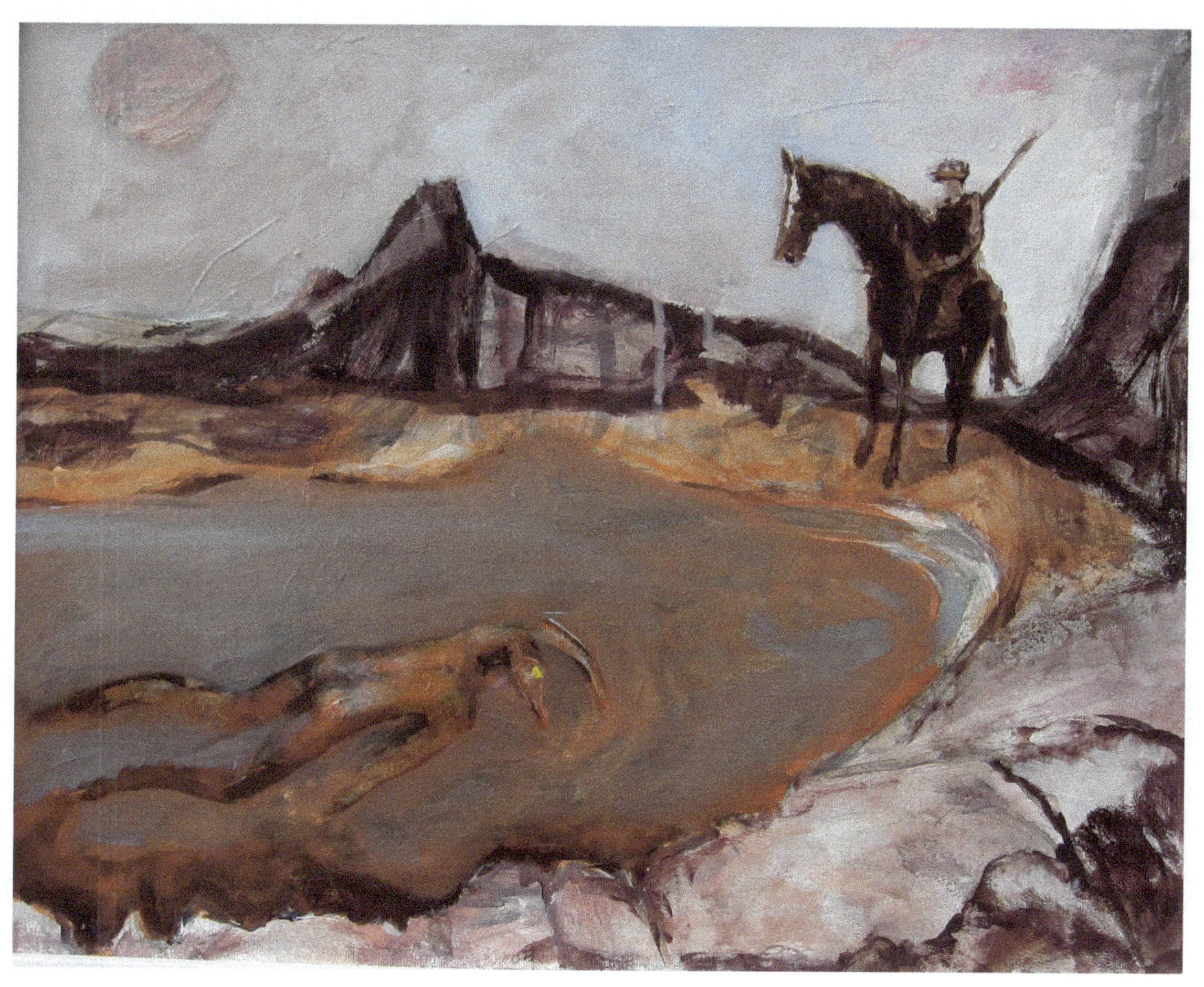

Swimming in Anzac Cove
41 x 51 cm
acrylic on canvas board

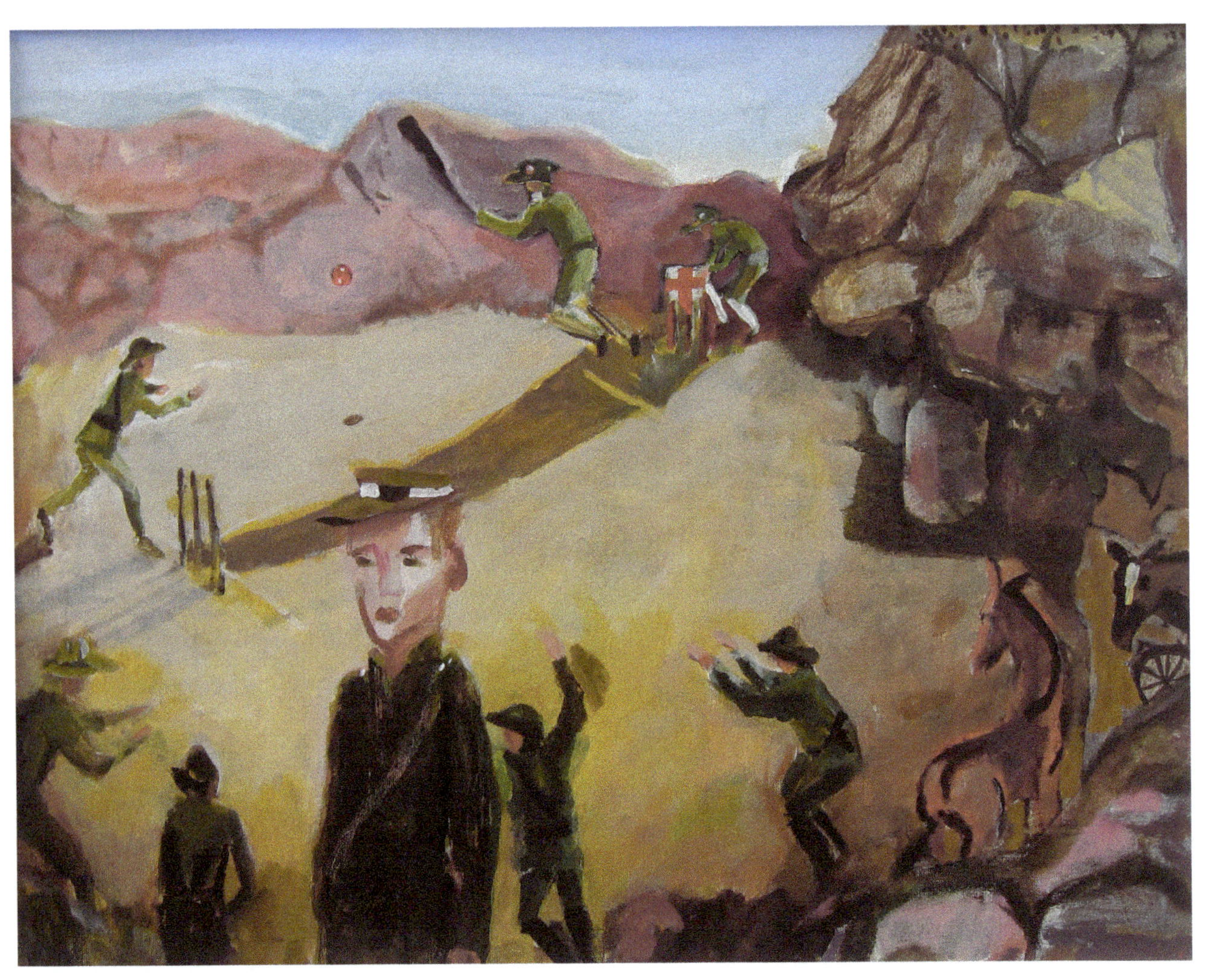

The Ruse Cricket Game
41 x 51 cm
acrylic on canvas board

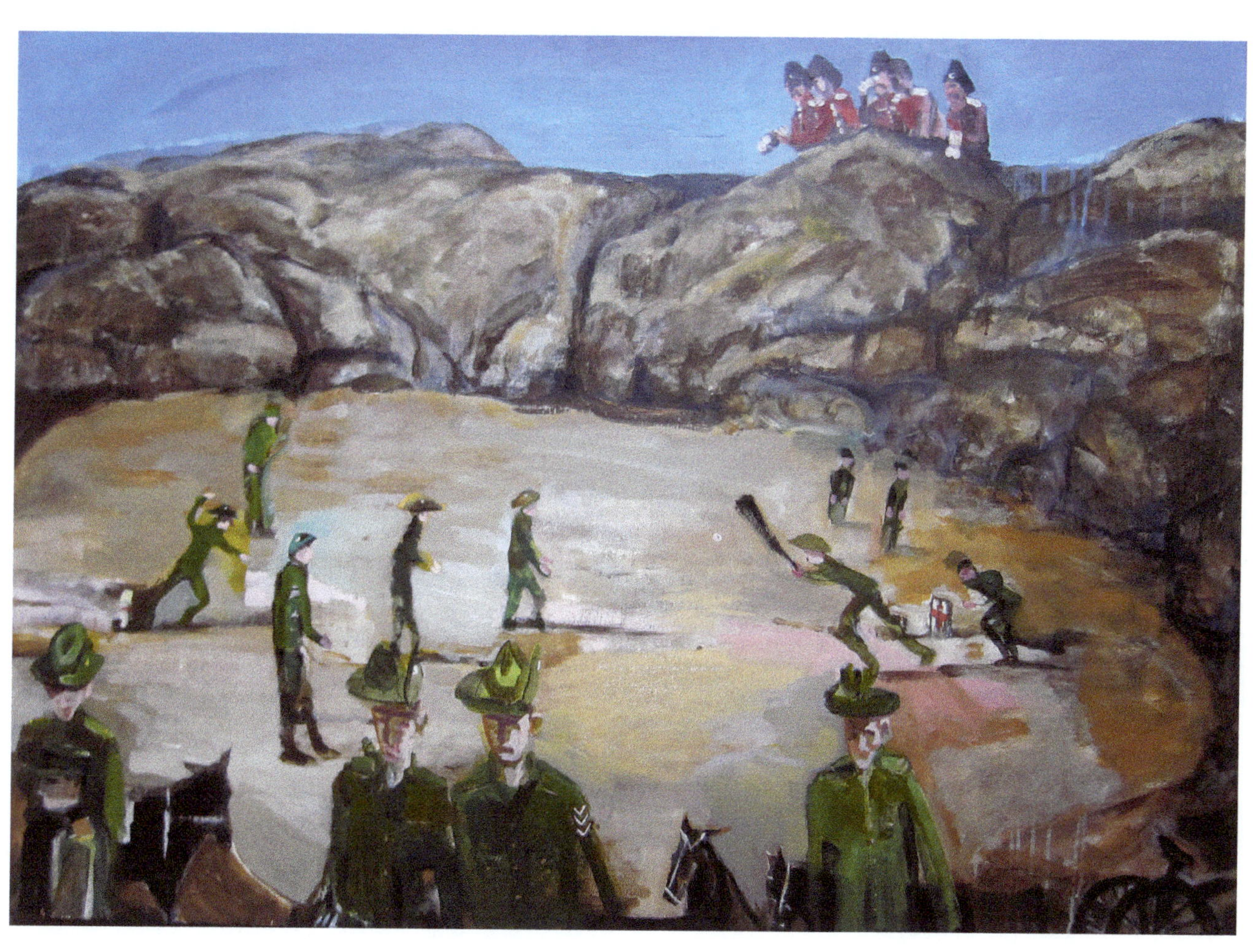

Cricket
80 x 110 cm
acrylic on board

Someone laughed loudly. Lots of us laughed, some smiled, some shouted derisively advising the far-away Turks where to aim. .. on shore among huge stacks of ammunition and stores. Men were bathing—so strange it seemed that men were dying too. Men were toiling among the heavy stacks of stores, men trudged all over that tiny beach in ragged, clay-stained uniforms, their familiar Australian faces cheerful and grimy under sprouting beards.

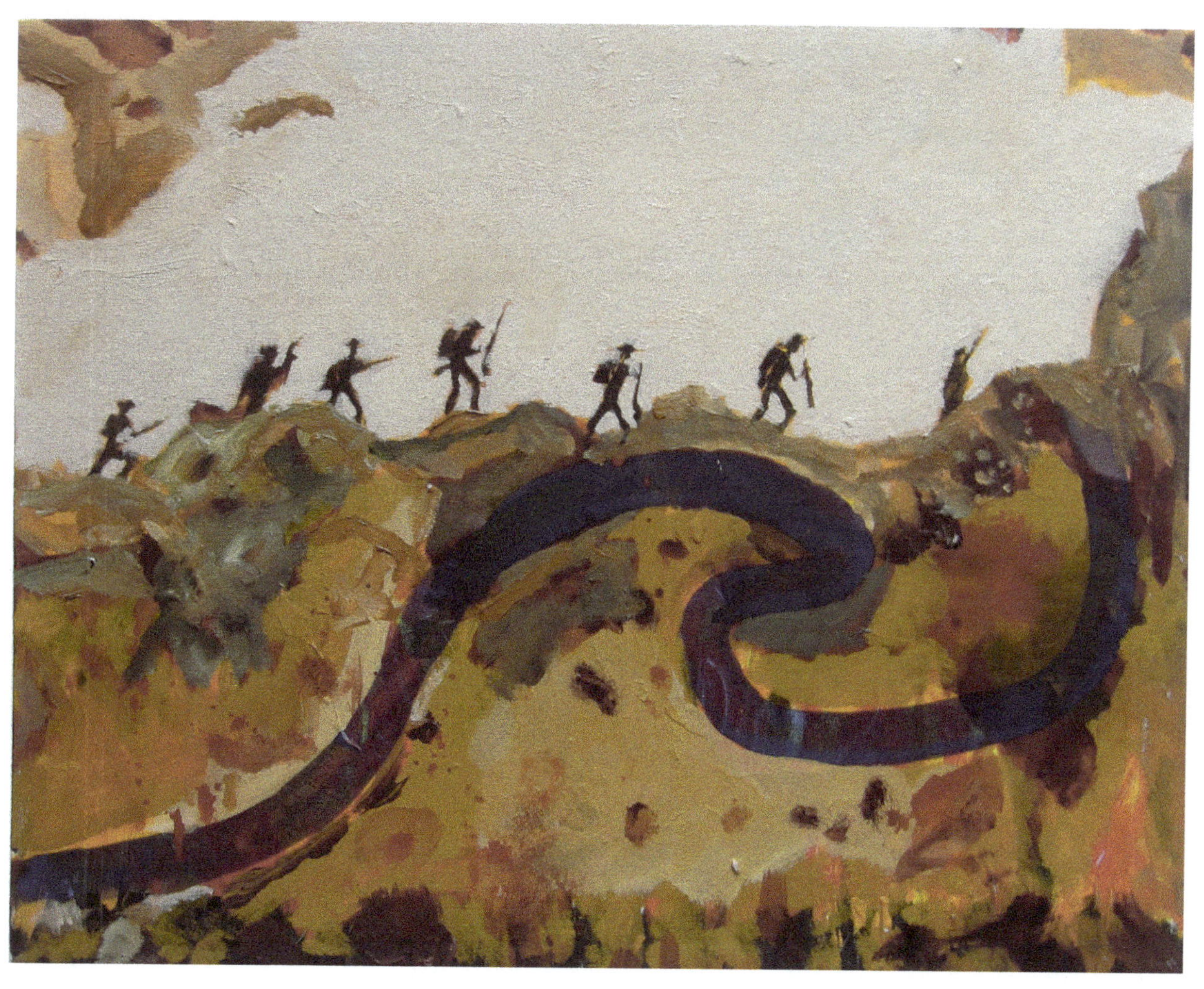

Leaving
41 x 51 cm
acrylic on canvas board

Strange! a few birds are flying about, merrily chirping, while the air is trilling with death!

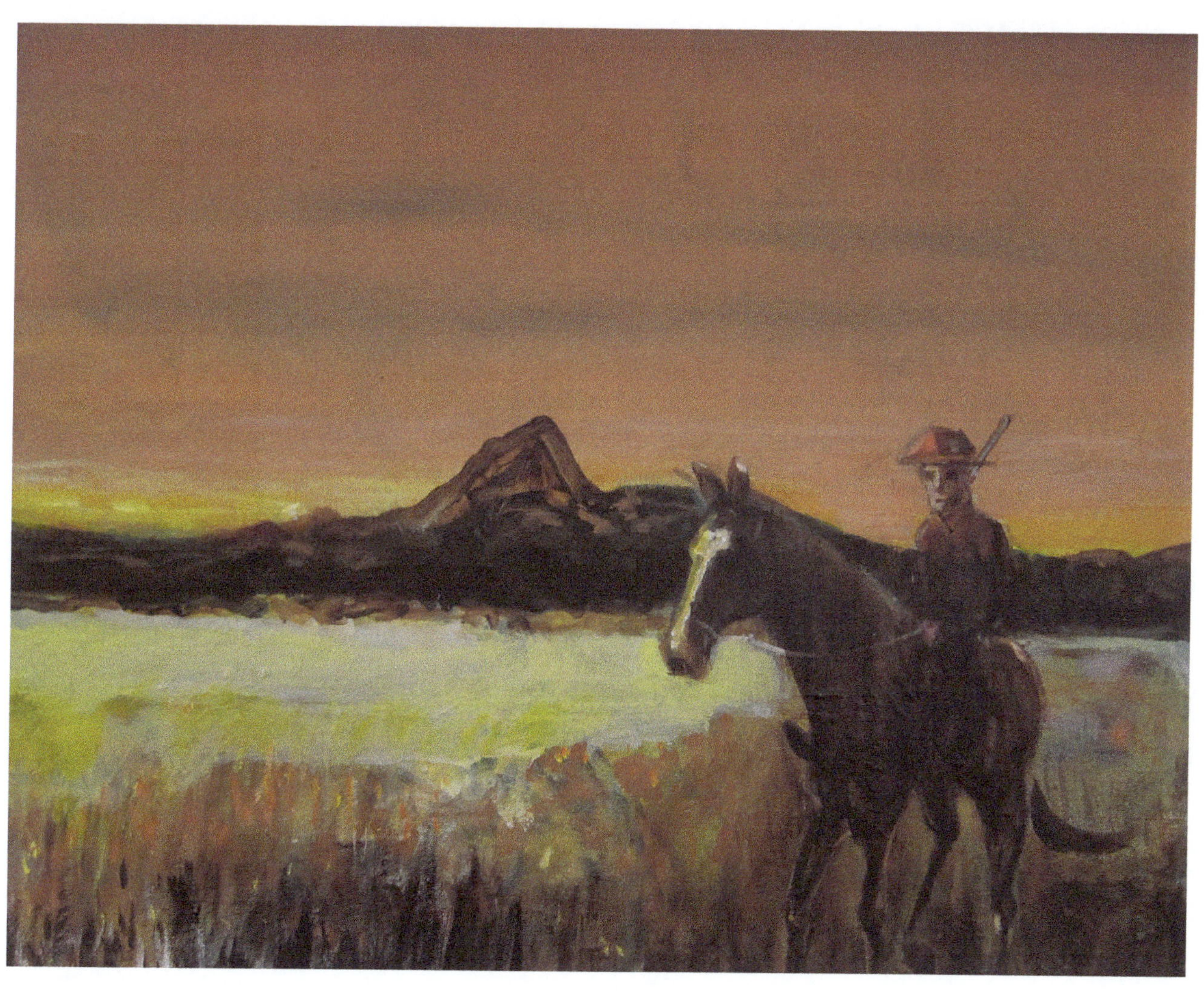

Lone Guard
41 x 51 cm
acrylic on canvas board

Last night, a P.&O. boat glided past; we could feel her engines throbbing... like the heart-beats of a mammoth out of breath. She just glided by so close, so brilliantly lit up, that we almost imagined ourselves lounging on her deck-chairs. Some of the passengers coo-eed to us and shouted: “Go it, Australia!”

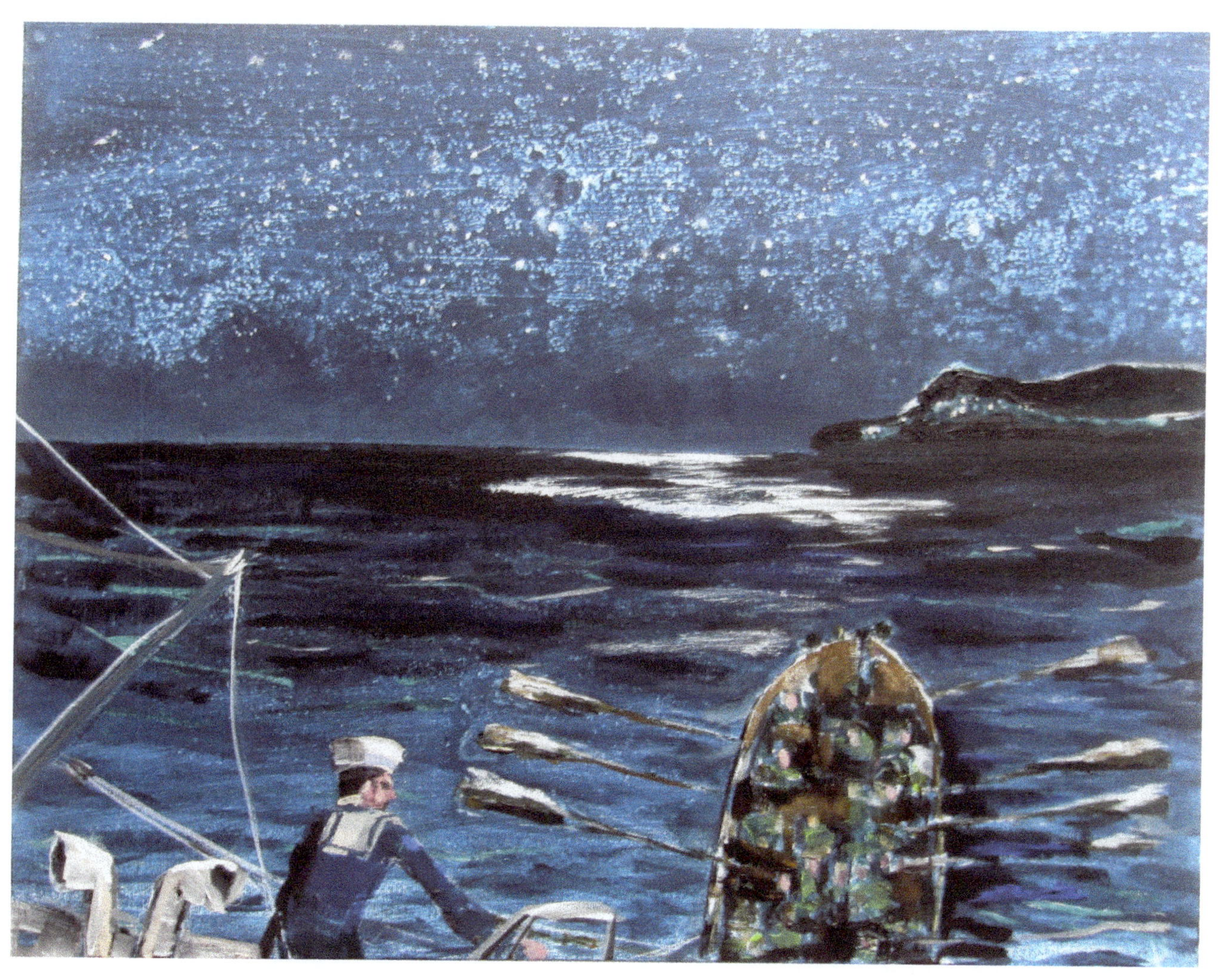

The Evacuation
41 x 51 cm
acrylic on canvas board

It got coldly dark. If a man were home he'd be just at the sliprails letting go his horse before he went in to tea. Or a city man would be pushing open the garden gate. Bang! bang! whizz whizz, zip, zip, zip, zip, bang! zip, zipp, bang! bang! bang!—Hell's orchestra, with additions, as the shrapnel burst in vicious balls of flame within the hollow basin: on the sides of the hills: above the hills—everywhere!

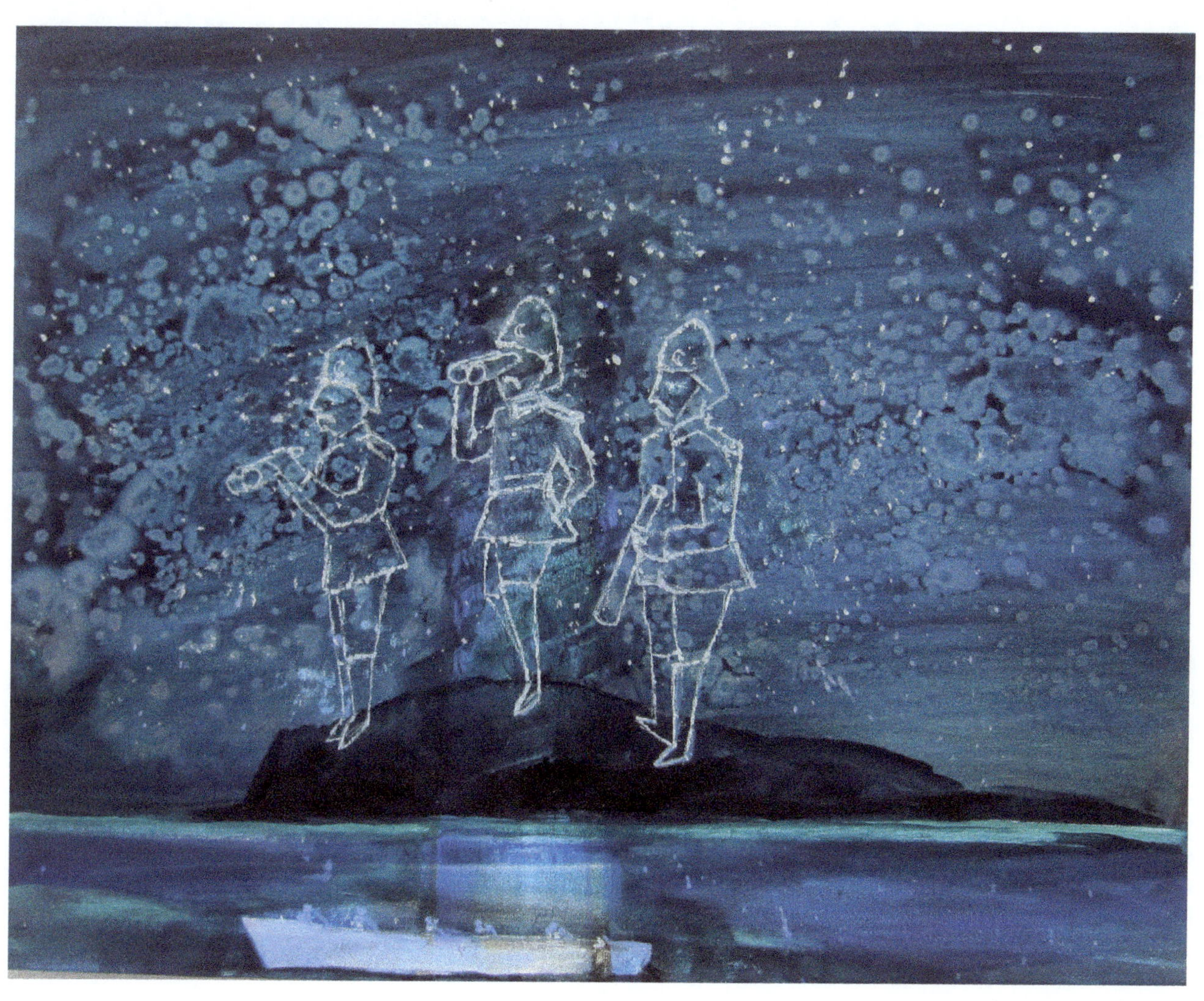

Turks Watching
41 x 51 cm
acrylic on canvas board

Up jumped Bertie, chucked his hands above his head and somersaulted, let out an awful screech, and howling something about his "Scotch blood stirring" sped away towards the advancing pipers. Nix and Morry and Stan and I followed and met the pipers and drummers coming down the track.

A rollicking crowd was following them up: the pipers piped the silly beggars home, Bertie yelling as he did a clan dance in advance.

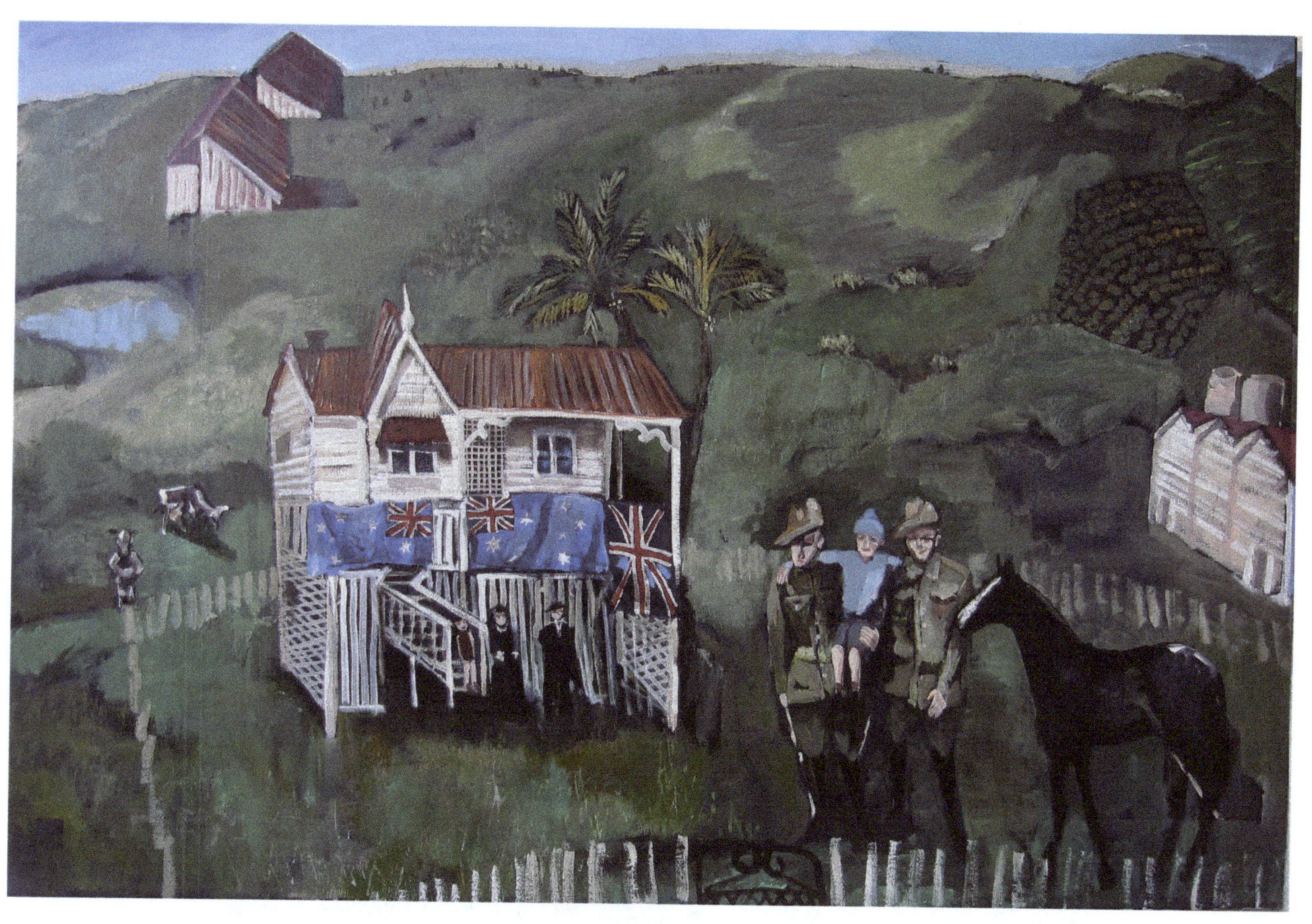

Home
80 x 110 cm
acrylic on board

The Author

Ion Idriess was born in Sydney in 1889, and brought up in Tenterfield and Broken Hill. He searched for opal at Lightning Ridge and gold in Queensland. With the outbreak of war in 1914, he enlisted in the 5th Light Horse Regiment, AIF, as a trooper and was wounded at Gallipoli where he acted as a spotter for the sniper Billy Sing. Idriess saw action in Palestine, Sinai and Turkey and was wounded at Beersheba. In 1919 he travelled to Cape York, and worked with pearlers and missionaries in the Torres Strait islands and Papua New Guinea. Gold mining and opal gouging intrigued him, as did buffalo shooting in the Northern Territory, and journeys to Central and Western Australia. He published widely from 1927 to 1969, with over 50 books, notably *Prospecting for Gold* and *Lasseter's Last Ride* (both 1931), *The Desert Column* and *Flynn of the Inland* (both 1932), *Drums of Mer* and *Gold-Dust and Ashe*s (both 1933) and The Cattle King and *Man Tracks* (both 1935). ETT Imprint has 32 of his books in print, including his memoir of WW1 aviators – *Our Flying Aces.*

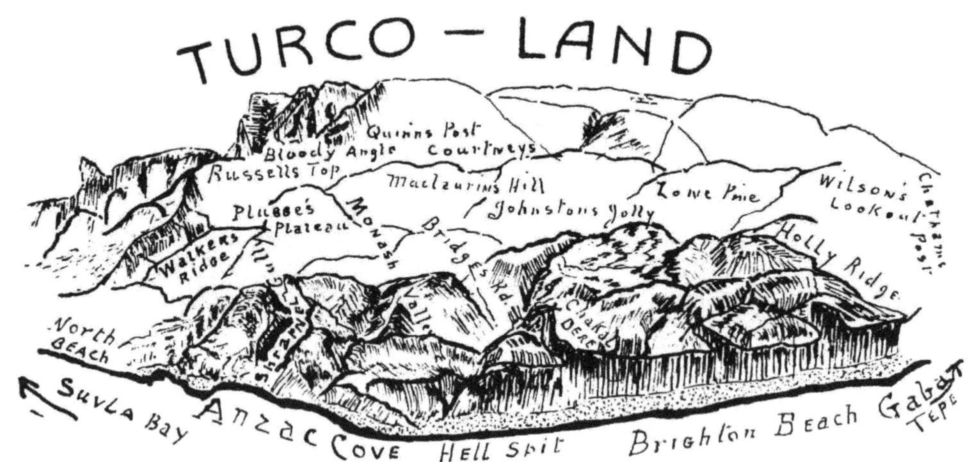

The author's impression of Gallipoli.

The Artist

Artist Geoff Harvey was born in 1954 and staged his first solo exhibition at Rex Irwin in 1977. He has held 25 solo exhibitions at Robin Gibson in Sydney since 1985. His paintings and sculpture have won the Blake Prize, Sculpture by the Sea Prize, the Muswellbrook Painting Prize, and the Gallipoli Art Prize twice. His father was stationed in New Guinea aged 16 during World War 2, and his early student art work revolved around the personal history paintings of his father's life. "Many aspects of the story of Gallipoli fascinated me from an early age," Harvey has said. "I did not study art at school but I did illustrate my history assignments with many drawings. The Gallipoli campaign was one I spent countless hours doing."

Forgotten Heroes, by Geoff Harvey. Gallipoli Art Prize 2020 (courtesy Gallipoli Club

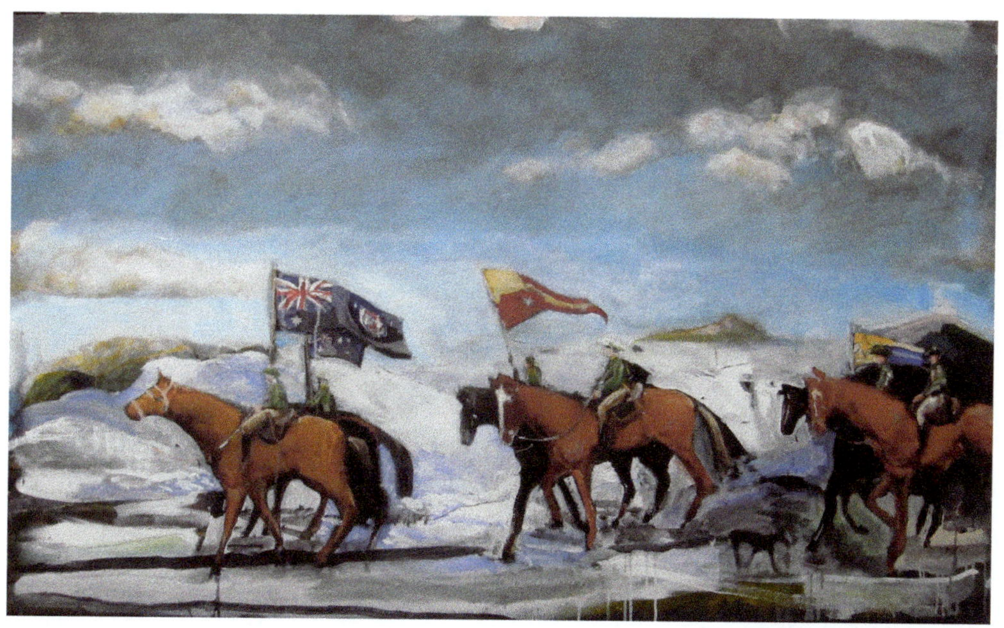

Printed in Australia
AUHW011126140422
362322AU00005B/5

9 781922 698223